Good Dad's Guide To Pregnancy

Honest Advice, Funny Stories, and Practical Wisdom for First-Time Fathers

Ben Clardy

Contents

Dedication

My dad, like all *good dads*, was not perfect. He made plenty of mistakes, some of which I know weighed heavily on him. He carried those mistakes with humility — not as marks of failure, but as reminders to keep striving to do better.

He worked hard to provide for us. Despite this, he always found his way to school plays, the soccer sidelines, and the dinner table. When life got messy, as it inevitably does, he didn't leave. He stayed. That steadfast presence made the world feel safe.

Dad would often refer to me as his *"favorite son."* I'm his only son, of course — but that was Dad. Always quick with a joke, he's undoubtedly the influence behind my habit of reaching for humor when plain words fall short.

It was only when I found myself standing in his shoes that I began to understand the weight he carried, and the grace with which he carried it. What once seemed ordinary now feels extraordinary.

Any strength I bring to my role as a father, any wisdom I manage to pass on — it all traces back to him. He showed me what it means to be a man who stands for his family and leads with love. He set the foundation. The rest is just me trying to build on it.

This book is dedicated to my father — whose quiet strength, unwavering presence, and everyday acts of love shaped my understanding of what it means to be a *good dad*.

Thank you, Dad, for showing me the way.

~Your *"favorite"* Son, Ben

Introduction

Since you're reading this book, it's fairly safe to assume that you have either successfully impregnated a woman or are dangerously close to doing so. Either way, you will find yourself embarking on a self-inflicted journey for which no amount of education, training, or previous life experience could prepare you.

You, my friend, are about to become a dad.

I imagine that particular word — *"dad"* — may feel a bit foreign when heard in reference to yourself. Up until now, you've gone through the usual sequence of labels: *infant, toddler, kid, boy, teen, young man, man* — all standard indicators of your natural progression as a human male. But this next step? It's a doozy.

And yet, for a transition so monumental, it's surprising how easily one can become a dad. Any Y-chromosome-bearing human in the company of a willing woman and a free afternoon can achieve it. Happens all the time. In fact, 5-10 men worldwide will have become dads by the time you finish reading this paragraph. It's because of the relative ease with which fatherhood can begin that I want to make something abundantly clear...

This book isn't just about becoming a dad. You don't need my help with that. Instead, it's about raising the bar and using the next nine months or so to get a head start on becoming what I call, plainly and simply, a _good_ dad.

Why not a _"perfect dad"_, you may ask?

The answer is simple — they don't exist. If they did, they'd be mythical creatures. Something akin to Bigfoot, but sporting a BabyBjörn.

Perfection, simply put, is unattainable. It can only be reached after making every possible mistake and learning from each one. The obvious problem, of course, is that parenting never stops teaching you. There's always another curveball, another stage, another humbling reminder of how much you still don't know. The very idea of perfection is entirely at odds with the beautiful mess that parenting is. It's a collision of laughter and exhaustion, wonder and frustration, small miracles and colossal screw-ups. This is why, in my humble opinion, it makes far more sense to strive to be _good_, rather than perfect.

A _good dad_ is present. He shows up, he participates, and he does his best to anticipate his pregnant partner's needs. He listens when she needs to vent about pregnancy aches, mood swings, and her growing resentment toward stairs. He simply does what needs doing — whether that means rubbing swollen feet, assembling a crib whose instructions were seemingly translated from Klingon, or making spontaneous grocery store runs to feed her newly developed but insatiable appetite for Mini-Mars Bars.

Introduction

Being a *good dad* doesn't mean you won't make mistakes. You will. Quite often, in fact. There will be times when you'll say the wrong thing, think the wrong thing, and do the wrong thing, but as long as you keep putting in the effort and striving to do a little better on the next attempt, you'll inevitably become exactly what your partner and child need you to be.

This is why *good* is the goal.

If you're wondering how I acquired such vast depths of scholarly wisdom, allow me to introduce myself...

My name is Ben.

Approximately nine months before our daughter was born, I made what doctors refer to as a *"significant biological contribution."* My lovely wife, Tambi, refers to this event as *"the easy part."* Over the next 3 trimesters, both she and I experienced our own versions of extreme human transformation. Hers mostly physical. Mine more psychological.

Take, for instance, the fateful Tuesday evening in our second trimester when Tambi sent me to the store for pickles. A simple errand, you might think. But this wasn't just any pickle-procuring mission. This was a precisely defined quest for *"the garlic dill spears, but only the Claussen ones in the refrigerated section, not those imposters on the regular shelf, and under <u>no circumstances</u> should I return home with hamburger chips."* Pre-pregnancy Ben would have grabbed the first jar with a picture of a pickle on it and called it a day. But, *good dad*, Ben? He perused that grocery aisle for seventeen minutes, comparing jars, sending photos for approval, and ignoring the pitying looks from store employees who had undoubtedly witnessed this exact scenario play out countless times before. When

I finally returned home, triumphant with precisely the correct jar of pickles, Tambi looked up from the couch, smiled sweetly, and said, *"I'm going to bed."* It was experiences such as these that contributed so meaningfully to my rapid transformation into a *good dad*.

Our pregnancy was, by medical standards, entirely *"typical"* — a term that can be rather misleading. The first trimester taught me that sympathetic nausea is quite real. This discovery was made while holding back her hair at 5 AM and failing to avoid the inadvertent inhalation of lingering vomit fumes. The second trimester granted a merciful reprieve, lulling us into a false sense of security, which had me thinking, *"Well, that wasn't so bad!"* — with the naive optimism of someone complacently paddling a canoe towards a waterfall. Then came the third trimester, where I discovered my previously unknown talent for interpreting grunts, sighs, and moans as cave-womanesque instructions for arranging supportive bed pillows into an assortment of architecturally impossible, baby-belly-supporting configurations. I nested like a deranged bird. I cleaned 436 linear feet of baseboards. I assembled baby furniture with an intensity that suggested the survival of our species depended entirely on the correct placement of Shelf B into Slot C.

For whatever reason, I stepped into my new role with both feet. Sure, it was weird, awkward, and challenging on a variety of levels, but after nine months of procuring pickles, periodic puking, pillow piles, and paternal preparations, our reward was the arrival of Molly — a happy, healthy, red-headed baby girl who, in a merciful twist of genetic fortune, looks just like her mother. In the end, it turns out that the midnight snack runs, the furniture assembly marathons, and the baseboards scrubbed to an unnatural gleam were more than worth it. Not just for the daughter we love and adore, but for the *good dad* I became in the process.

Introduction

So, *"Why write this book?*, you might ask.

When I initially found myself teetering on the precipice of impending dad-dom, I became a voracious reader of baby books, parenting books, and anything that might compensate for my distinct lack of innate fatherly instinct. It was during this time that I noticed something peculiar about the books written for soon-to-be dads. They seemed to fall into two polar-opposite ends of a spectrum, with not much in the middle.

At one end were the clinical guides, which read like medical textbooks. These books were informative, sure, but about as engaging as an instruction manual for a toaster. They provided a wealth of medical knowledge, but they did precious little to prepare me for the sheer spectacle of pregnancy — the drama, the unpredictability, and the weirdly wonderful chaos of it all. While helpful, these books left me hungry for connection, relevance, and genuine relatability.

Then, on the other end, were the books that operated under the assumption that dads are a subspecies of adult who must be addressed with the same gentle condescension one might use while explaining long division to a golden retriever. These books offered dads hearty pats on the head for accomplishing basic tasks, as if successfully not passing out during a routine ultrasound was on par with completing Navy SEAL training. *"Look who's being a helper!"* they seemed to say, with the unspoken understanding that *"helper"* is the ceiling of your potential contribution, not the floor.

It was observing this gaping void in practical dad knowledge that lit the fire under me. I figured if I could stumble my way through the pregnancy maze and come out the other side intact, then perhaps my missteps, awkward victories, and half-decent insights could help other soon-to-be-dads do the same. So, I wrote the book I wish I'd had.

While this book's primary goal is to help you become a *good dad*, it will do so with a white-knuckle grasp on the hysterics of the journey. You'll encounter heaping helpings of self-deprecating humor because, for one thing, I can't help it. For another, I can think of no better means of communicating the gravity of such a profound experience that seems to consist of equal parts miracle and circus.

For example, you'll learn such practical nuggets as:

- How to survive prenatal appointments without saying something so catastrophically nonsensical that the OB-GYN writes it down for inclusion in their memoir.
- How to decode pregnancy cravings and determine whether this is genuinely worth a drive across town or if offering an alternative might result in your personal belongings appearing on the front lawn.
- How to develop the ability to identify and eliminate household odors that suddenly trigger nausea, even when said odors are imperceptible to the non-knocked-up human nose.
- How to support your pregnant partner in ways that might — *just might* — prevent her from contemplating your murder around month eight when you innocently point out that her feet happen to resemble over-filled water balloons.

You'll also get timely updates concerning the growth and development of your wee one, helpful advice for various tasks and preparations that should be made at specific milestones along the way, and potentially — *most helpful of all* — blatantly listing out a wide variety of things you should absolutely avoid saying or doing that could jeopardize your good standing with your *(increasingly)* significant-other.

Pregnancy, in many ways, could be compared to a nine-month-long roller coaster ride designed by someone with a questionable understanding of human comfort and a complete disregard for the laws of physics. You are strapped in beside your partner, though her seat is fully loaded with snazzy features such as nausea, heartburn, body aches, mood swings, and the ever-increasing sensation of her internal organs being used as a trampoline.

This roller coaster ride will consist of all manner of twists, loops, drops, and memorable experiences around every turn. Such as how your partner's body will change in ways that defy explanation and eventually produce its own localized gravitational pull. You'll find yourself developing strong opinions about stroller engineering and crib safety ratings. You'll have heated discussions about baby names and their potential for playground mockery. You'll become intimately familiar with terms like *"effacement," "dilation,"* and *"colostrum"* — words that previously had no place in your vocabulary, but will now feature prominently in dinner conversations that make your childless friends suddenly recall urgent appointments elsewhere.

And through all of this, you'll be presented with a simple, recurring choice that will ultimately determine whether you earn the prestigious title of *"good dad"*...

Will you *step up*, or will you *check out*?

Strip away the jokes, the funny stories, and valiant attempts at humor, and what you're left with is the heart of this book. It exists solely to help you make this choice — for your partner, your child, and yourself.

So welcome to the madness, my friend. This will likely be the most bewildering, exhilarating, terrifying, and rewarding nine months of your life. The roller coaster is now in motion. Please keep your arms inside the cart at all times. Things are going to get a little crazy, but remember:

It's nothing that a *good dad* can't handle.

THE FIRST TRIMESTER

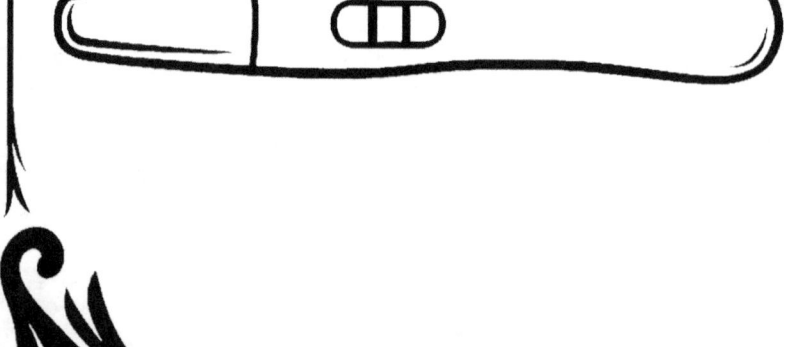

This is the opening act of pregnancy, where you, dear reader, begin your slow transformation from ordinary human male to a strange, limbo-dwelling creature, typically referred to as *"an expectant father."*

In terms of milestones, this is the trimester of discovery. It begins with a plastic stick that, when moistened with the urine of an impregnanted female, instantly changes the course of your entire existence.

Your role in the early weeks can feel abstract at times — there's no visible bump, no kicks to feel, just an invisible science experiment taking place beneath her waistband. But trust me, the work is already well under way.

So take a breath. You're in it now, and while you don't need to be perfect, you do need to be present, patient, and ready to adapt to the strange new world of trimester one.

BABY SIZE
WEEK 1
"the dot of an *i*"

future diaper
destroyer

Chapter 1

Weeks 1-4

The Bombshell

It was a perfectly ordinary Tuesday evening. The kind that slips quietly into the category of *"forgettable,"* which made it the ideal setting for a life-altering revelation.

The lights were dim, the dishwasher was humming in the background, and I was sitting on the living room couch, watching a dumb reality show about people who marry complete strangers. Exactly the type of thing you watch when your life is merrily cruising along on autopilot.

Unbeknownst to me, my wife, Tambi, was in the bathroom, urinating on a plastic stick. Activator pad moistened, she lay the stick on the counter, resting it carefully on a few folded squares of toilet paper. She then leaned in and watched as the little window slowly worked to reveal its verdict...

Two unmistakable pink lines.

She stared at the results for a long moment, wondering if they might change if she gave them enough time. But the lines stayed — steady, absolute, undeniable. With an informational bombshell now loaded in her brain, she stood, turned, opened the door, departed from the bathroom, walked down the hallway toward the living room, and then stopped next to the couch.

The bomb bay doors were open. The payload was primed. Target sighted. She didn't preface it with any kind of emotional buffer. Instead, she simply pulled the lever.

"I'm pregnant."

Fortunately, I had mentally rehearsed for this very moment countless times before. In my fantasies, I was dashingly prepared. The kind of man who sweeps his wife off her feet, twirling her around in circles, tears of joy streaming down our faces as I deliver an impromptu speech worthy of a romantic movie's final scene.

What actually happened was a tad less cinematic.

I stared at her and blinked.

My brain, which only moments earlier had been contentedly processing the drama of reality TV, decided to temporarily disconnect from my body. My jaw slowly opened as if to speak. She patiently waited for words, but none came out. My lovely wife later told me she was genuinely concerned that I was having a stroke.

Eventually, reality came crashing back in.

I was going to be a dad?

A dad.

A DAD.

The word *"dad"* ping-ponged around my skull like a screensaver, occasionally hitting a corner and pinging off in a new direction.

Dad. Father. Parent. The official and wholly responsible guardian of a tiny, sentient human being.

The emotions hit me in waves: excitement *(holy cow, we're having a baby!)*, panic *(holy cow, we're having a baby!)*, pride *(I totally did that!)*, confusion *(how the heck did I do that?)*, terror *(what if the baby inherits my sense of humor?)*, wonder *(do babies toot in the womb?)*, and the sudden, horrifying, crushing realization that I knew precisely *nada* about raising children and had somehow blissfully gone a full twenty-six years without paying attention to how other humans successfully reared their young.

My brain, helpful as ever, chose this moment to remind me that the last living thing I'd been responsible for was a small, decorative cactus. The shriveled succulent, barely clinging to life, gives me condescending looks when I stroll by, well-fed and watered, all but oblivious to its neglected existence.

Processing the News

The first thing you need to know is that there is no *"right"* way to react to pregnancy news. Some guys burst into tears of joy. Some scream in excitement. Others enter a fugue state where they just keep nodding and repeat, *"Wow... wow... wow..."* on loop. One friend of mine started spontaneously cleaning the kitchen as if good countertop hygiene was suddenly the most pressing concern in the universe. As diverse as these reactions are, all are perfectly valid.

The important thing is that you get to the acceptance phase as quickly as possible. You're going to be a dad, after all, so it's time to shift from *"holy crap"* to *"let's do this!"*

A typical progression may go something like this:

Denial Phase: *"Nah. Can't be. Maybe the test was faulty? Maybe she's messing with me? Yeah, this is definitely a prank. She's hilarious."*

* She then produces a second positive test. And a third. And a fourth. (**Fun fact:** *It's for the purpose of quickly shattering one's position within the denial phase that pregnancy tests are often sold in bulk.)*

Fear Phase: *"Oh God, this is real. I'm not ready. I don't even know how to become a dad. Biologically, yes, but like... do I need to start wearing socks with sandals now? Should I begin practicing dad jokes? What's my stance on thermostat settings?"*

Acceptance Phase: *"Okay. I can do this. Other people have done this. Dumber people have done this. Smarter people, too, but so what? Even cave people did this without books or YouTube. I'll be fine. This is fine. Everything is fine."*

* What follows next is, perhaps, the most predictable and unavoidable phase of early pregnancy...

The Great Google Spiral: This is where you, a presumably well-functioning adult-ish person, suddenly become the type who questions all manner of baby-related fodder that would make a five-year-old seem sophisticated:

"is it dark in the womb"

"do babies get bored in there"

"baby head VS vagina"

"how do babies breathe while inside another person"

Your browser history becomes a fascinating chronicle of diminishing coherence as you make your first foray into attaining

4

valuable pregnancy knowledge. ***Pro tip:*** Maybe don't search *"what does childbirth look like"* before bed. The sleepless nights will be here soon enough, my friend. There's no need to rush it.

Telling People Or Not

Once you've absorbed the news and cleared your browser history of increasingly desperate baby-related searches, you might feel an overwhelming urge to tell people. But before you grab a megaphone and start making announcements, take a breath.

Many couples choose to hold off on sharing the news, and with good reason. The first trimester carries the highest risk of miscarriage — a heartbreaking reality that no one wants to dwell on but should be acknowledged. While most pregnancies progress without issue, some parents-to-be prefer to wait until the second trimester, when the risk drops significantly, before looping in friends, family, and the wider world.

This is a deeply personal decision, and there's no right or wrong answer. Some couples tell a small, trusted circle right away for support, while others keep it entirely private until they feel more confident about the pregnancy. If you're unsure what to do, follow your partner's lead. She's the one growing the new human, after all, so her preferences should take priority.

That being said, when you do start telling people, here are some considerations of who you might tell first and how they may react:

Your Parents: Their reaction will often fall into one of two extremes — *ecstatic joy* or *mild panic*. They'll either start picking out grandparent names before you finish your sentence (*"Nana? Grandma? Ooh, what about Gigi?"*), or they'll sigh deeply while

5

staring at old photos of you, as if mentally reviewing every questionable decision you've ever made.

Your Siblings: If they don't have kids, expect a mix of excitement and disbelief that *you*, of all people, are soon to be responsible for another human life. If they have kids, prepare for smug grins, sarcastic comments, and cryptic warnings about sleep deprivation.

Friends Without Kids: They'll congratulate you while wearing the expression of someone watching a man unknowingly wander into a lion enclosure — half excitement, half curiosity. They'll keep inviting you to things, but with the same expectations one has when sending a party invitation to a cousin who lives in Bermuda.

Friends With Kids: They've been waiting for this moment. They'll smirk, slap you on the back, and say, *"Dude, welcome to the club,"* with the barely concealed glee of someone who knows what's coming but refuses to spoil the surprise. Then, without any further prompting, they'll launch into a rapid-fire barrage of unsolicited advice: the best baby monitors, the only sleep training method that *"actually works,"* the car seat they swear by, the stroller they regret buying, and the brand of diapers that allegedly changed their lives.

Your Boss: If your job will be affected by this (*hello, paternity leave*), you'll eventually need to inform them. Most people choose to wait until the second trimester, but sometimes secrecy is impossible. When you do have the conversation, your boss's reaction will likely fall into one of three categories:

- **The Supportive Boss:** *"That's amazing! Family comes first. Let's talk about your leave and how we can support you."* (*You may momentarily consider naming the baby after them.*)

6

- **The All-Business Boss:** *"Congrats. Now, let's discuss coverage while you're out so things don't fall through the cracks."* (*No nonsense, no emotion, just logistics. You respect it.*)
- **The Slightly Panicked Boss:** *"Oh... uh... wow. So... like... how much time will you need off? A week? Two? THREE!?"* (*They are now mentally reworking the entire company schedule while making a poor attempt to smile through it.*)

Regardless of their response, your best move is to come in with a plan. Know your company's paternity leave policy, have a rough timeline in mind, and reassure them that you're not about to vanish into fatherhood without a trace.

Your Co-workers: The ones with kids will pat you on the back like a soldier heading into battle and say things like, *"Better sleep while you can, man."* The ones without kids will nod politely, offer a generic *"Congratulations!"* while making a mental note to refresh their birth control supply.

The World: Social media announcements come last, not first. Your grandma should not find out she's going to be a great-grandmother via a Facebook post. Once the news is public, prepare for an avalanche of opinions, unsolicited parenting advice, and people you haven't spoken to in years suddenly feeling the need to weigh in.

First Doctors Appointment

You will sit in a room with a doctor or midwife and hear words you don't understand, like *"hCG levels"* and *"fundal height."* You'll nod sagely while internally wondering if they're legitimately speaking a different language or if your brain has simply decided to stop processing certain categories of words.

Just keep in mind that the main goals of this particular appointment are to confirm the pregnancy and determine an approximate due date. Don't stress if you feel a bit unprepared. You'll get much better as time goes on, I assure you.

The Important Stuff

1) **Show up**: You are required to be there. No exceptions. Even if the world is ending, you had better be in that examination room. This is your first official opportunity to show your pregnant partner that you're 100% *in this,* and also one of the preliminary steps of building your *good dad* cred. Don't miss it.

2) **Take notes**: Trust me, you will forget 90% of what the doctor says within five minutes, if not sooner. Your partner will ask you later what the doctor said about something specific, and you'll realize you spent that entire portion of the conversation wondering if in utero babies can sneeze.

3) **Act like you understand**: Nod and say things like *"Ah, yes, that makes sense."* Also, as previously mentioned, do refrain from asking the Doctor whether in utero babies can sneeze. They can't, and the Doc will form a doubtful opinion of you. Instead, consider asking questions like:

– *When is the estimated due date?*

– *Are there any risks or concerns right now?*

– *What should we be focusing on until the next appointment?*

These questions show you're engaged *and* mentally present, which will earn you points and reassurance. They also make you seem like you're not just a guy who wandered into the wrong exam room while looking for the vending machine.

Don't Be That Guy

The fact that you're willingly reading a pregnancy book means that the following content likely does not apply to you. Still, for the sake of posterity, I will issue a stark warning:

Please, do not be *"That Guy."*

That Guy is the antithesis of a *good dad*. He's the type who refuses to take pregnancy seriously, treats it like an inconvenience, or thinks his primary involvement will be to pass out cigars in the waiting room like it's 1953. He feels as though pregnancy is *"the woman's job"* and has no genuine interest in becoming a *good dad*.

Signs You May Be *"That Guy"*:

- *You refer to the baby as "it" or, worse, "the situation".*

- *You think your primary role is "moral support."*

- *Your idea of baby-proofing is putting the X-Box on a higher shelf.*

If any of this sounds uncomfortably familiar, I strongly encourage you to stop reading, close this book, and grasp it firmly between both hands. Then, with great determination, use it to repeatedly whack yourself in the forehead until a more enlightened perspective takes hold. This practice, in scientific circles, is commonly referred to as *"an attitude adjustment."* I suggest getting it out of the way now before your aggravated, uncomfortable, hormone-fueled partner takes matters into her own hands.

Baby Status Update

At week one, your baby is roughly the size of the dot on this "i." Take a second and really look closely at that dot. Astounding, isn't it? Within that wildly ambitious cluster of multiplying cells is the blueprint for a complete, fully functioning human being with eventual opinions about baby food flavors and an irrational hatred of car seats. And it doesn't stay small for long. By week four, your baby is rapidly approaching the size of a BB — the kind you'd load into a Red Ryder and promptly receive stern warnings to avoid shooting your eye out.

There's no heartbeat yet. No arms. No face. Just a tiny, spherical ball of cells. And yet, your baby's development is all very much underway. Cell division is happening at an insane pace. Chromosomes are locking into place. This microscopic miracle is already deciding things like hair color, eye shape, and whether they'll inherit your partner's musical tastes or perhaps your inexplicable talent for remembering obscure movie quotes.

This is where the story begins. Quietly. Invisibly. But undeniably underway.

Action Steps

The early weeks are your foundation for the pregnancy journey ahead. While you might still be processing the news, there are some critical things to put in motion right now.

Book that first prenatal appointment. If it hasn't been done, call her OB-GYN office or midwifery practice this week — don't delay. Ask specifically for the *"confirmation of pregnancy"* or *"first prenatal"* appointment. If she doesn't have an established provider, research ones that accept your insurance, have privileges at your preferred hospital, and have good reviews for their approach to birth.

Get in sync. Set up a shared calendar app on both your phones that automatically syncs appointments. Google Calendar, Apple Calendar, or apps like Cozi designed for families tend to work well. Make this digital hub the command center for all pregnancy-related dates. Add any appointments, events, or important milestones to both of your calendars. This will help you both stay on track.

Buy high-quality prenatal vitamins. Look for ones containing at least 400mcg of folic acid, 27mg of iron, 400mg of DHA, and 600 IU of vitamin D. If she's experiencing nausea, try gummies, taking them with food, or right before bed. Set up a designated spot where she'll see them daily *(next to her toothbrush or coffee maker)*, and implement a reminder system you both manage. Check with her doctor about any prescription prenatal vitamins that might be better absorbed or covered by insurance. While you're at it, evaluate your own vitamin routine. Supporting her health means maintaining yours, too.

Conduct a thorough insurance audit. Pull up your benefits portal today and locate the maternity coverage section. Identify your deductible, out-of-pocket maximum, and coverage percentages for prenatal visits, ultrasounds, genetic testing, and hospital delivery. Call your insurance provider with specific questions, such as:

- *Is pre-authorization required for certain tests?*
- *Which hospitals in your network have labor and delivery units?*
- *What's the process and deadline for adding your baby to your policy after birth?*

Create a spreadsheet tracking expected costs throughout pregnancy, and start setting aside funds now for any significant out-of-pocket expenses, especially if your deductible resets during her pregnancy.

Implement household health upgrades. Start by removing the obvious toxins. If you haven't already, swap out harsh cleaning products for pregnancy-safe alternatives — especially anything with strong fumes or weird chemical names you can't pronounce. Take over cat litter duty immediately to avoid the risk of toxoplasmosis. Organize the refrigerator so the healthy snacks are front and center, and the less-healthy options are either hidden behind a hearty head of lettuce or removed entirely.

And now, let's talk about smoking. If you smoke, this is an excellent time to quit. Secondhand smoke can seriously affect placental development, fetal growth, and birth outcomes. Even thirdhand smoke — the residue that clings to clothes, furniture, or hair — can pose risks. If there was ever a moment in your life to draw a hard line and say, *"I'm done,"* this is it. Quitting isn't easy, but becoming a father is one of the best reasons you'll ever have to do it. Not just for her. Not just for the baby. For your family.

Next, alcohol. A cold beer after a long day can be amazing, but if your partner's giving up alcohol entirely, then slamming IPAs on the couch while she sips lemon water isn't exactly a gesture of solidarity. If you want to have a drink, be courteous about it. Designate time to go out with friends. Keep it out of the house. Don't let drinking become something she sees or smells while she's giving up something for the sake of the baby. Support doesn't always come in the form of flowers or foot rubs. Sometimes, it looks like abstaining from alcohol because you realize how unfair it feels for her to watch you enjoy what she can't.

Hydration, by the way, is a big deal too. Install a water filter and buy her one of those giant, obnoxious water bottles with time markings and passive-aggressive encouragement printed on the side. (*"Seriously, drink more water!"*, *"You literally need this to live!"*, *"You're disappointing the baby!"*) Then make it your mission to keep it filled without being asked.

These small acts send a powerful message: *I'm in this with you.*

Build your pregnancy knowledge base. Create a dedicated folder on your phone or computer with pregnancy resources and bookmarks. Download two apps: a clinical one that explains development *(like WebMD Pregnancy)* and a community-based one for real experiences *(like What to Expect)*. Start a running list of questions for the doctor, terms you don't understand, and symptoms to monitor. While it's essential to be educated, <u>do not go overboard</u>! It's easy to fall into the trap of over-analyzing and working yourself up. Remember, the general process of pregnancy is entirely automatic, so don't over-complicate it.

Cherish This Time

One important message I'd like for you to take to heart is that this experience — *while truly life-changing* — is fleeting. Therefore, I encourage you to document and preserve the journey as much as you can.

Take photos of the positive pregnancy test. Capture her still-flat stomach with a date written on it. Trust me, the contrast with later photos will be mind-boggling. Write down how you reacted when she told you, where you were, and what you said. Preserve the moment you first call each other *"Mom"* and *"Dad."* Pay attention to the small shifts happening right now, before the physical changes become apparent. The way she unconsciously rests her hand on her stomach during conversations, protecting something no one can see yet.

This beginning chapter isn't just biological groundwork — *it's the foundation of your family's story*. Let that sink in! These early weeks are significant, even if they're marked more by nausea and uncertainty than by visible evidence. Someday, long from now, you'll look back at these days with surprising fondness. It's all very much worth noting, worth honoring, worth remembering.

BABY SIZE
WEEK 5

"10mm socket"

greatness
starts small

Chapter 2
Weeks 5-8
Morning Sickness

In the early morning, just as consciousness began to take hold, I instinctively reached my arm across the bed to where Tambi usually lay. Her side was still warm, but vacant. For a few moments, I lay there motionless, listening for signs of her whereabouts. Then, in the distance, from behind the closed bathroom door, I heard it — the faint, but unmistakable sound of retching.

I approached the bathroom, gently opened the door, and there, hunched over the toilet in the loose embrace of a sweatshirt, was my wife, clinging to the rim of the bowl and heaving like a freshman at a frat party.

With all the confidence of a man who has never experienced pregnancy, I said:

"Are you okay?"

She slowly turned her head toward me, her eyes a mix of exhaustion and irritation, and said:

"I'm throwing up."

I nodded as if this was new information. I had read up on this, and to me, this seemed to be her first bout with morning sickness. A classic symptom of early pregnancy. Thankfully, one of the pregnancy books I had been skimming through in the evenings had provided me with the precise kernel of knowledge needed to provide quick relief to my ailing wife.

I pivoted 180 degrees, rushed to the kitchen, yanked open the pantry door, scanned the shelves, and spotted the familiar white and blue box. Saltines — the holy grail of nausea management.

I tore into the box, extracted a long plastic sleeve, fumbled with opening it, trying one end and then the other, and finally resorted to ripping it open with my teeth somewhere between the pantry and the hallway. A few crackers broke and scattered to the floor, but there was no time for cleanup. I was operating on raw instinct now — guided by the sheer determination to deliver the miracle cure my wife so desperately needed.

I rounded the corner into the bathroom, catching the doorjamb with one hand and slingshotting myself through the doorway, my sock-clad feet skidding to a halt next to my wife, who was still slumped over the toilet with her head resting on her forearm.

I quietly kneeled beside her, presenting the crackers with both hands as if offering them up to an ancient altar. She opened one eye, looked at the Saltines, and said...

I don't want..., (insert barfing sound) *...crackers".*

Noted. No crackers.

Then, as we sat there on the bathroom floor, a useless sleeve of crackers in hand, she turned toward me with an expression that can only be described as deep, personal disgust, and she said:

"You smell awful."

Now, to be clear, I had just woken up. I showered the night before and had not done anything particular between then and now to smell bad. I had not rolled around in garbage, I had not been recently sprayed by a skunk, nor was I the one who was actively in the process of reversing the natural course of last night's chicken parm. Yet, apparently, I smelled awful and seemed to be the direct cause of her current nauseated state.

Determined to pinpoint the offending odor, I launched a scorched-earth campaign of olfactory warfare. My preferred deodorant? *Banned.* Aftershave? *Evicted.* Body wash? *Exiled.* All were replaced with scentless counterparts, which, after years of smelling like *something*, made it deeply unsettling to suddenly smell like *nothing*. It was as if I had been scrubbed out of existence. I became a human void — a man-shaped absence of smell. At one point, I waved my arm in front of my face just to see if I still occupied physical space, only to realize that I now smelled precisely like a shadow.

On a different morning, Tambi asked me to change clothes because I *"smelled like fabric softener."* Ironically, she was referring to the fabric softener we had intentionally switched to the day before. Its scent, if you can call it that, is *"rain."*

Despite the relentless waves of nausea and the ever-growing list of forbidden smells, she knew I was doing everything I could to help her through it. She knew I was trying, which I've come to learn is the most important thing. Pregnancy has a way of forcing a level of teamwork and connection that goes beyond words, deepening your bond in ways you never expected. And I think that's why, in that particular moment, she looked up at me with her pretty blue eyes and said the sweetest thing.

"It's not you — it's your molecules."

I felt reassured.

Morning Sickness Management

Morning sickness is one of pregnancy's great mysteries. It's an unpredictable, unstoppable force that follows no known laws of nature. You might assume it only strikes in the morning. You'd be wrong. You might think certain foods are obvious triggers. Wrong again. The reality is it can be set off by anything at any time, and one of the biggest culprits? Scents.

There is often no rhyme or reason behind which smells become offensive. Something your partner has loved her entire life, like coffee, vanilla candles, or her favorite shampoo — can suddenly become as offensive as a sweaty wool sock with the sheep still attached. Meanwhile, inexplicably, other scents that would normally be considered objectively unpleasant may now be tolerated or even enjoyed. Pregnancy is weird like that.

Here are some tips:

Go Unscented: If she starts recoiling when you enter a room, you may need to de-fragrance yourself. This means switching to scent-free soap, scent-free shampoo, scent-free deodorant, and scent-free detergent. Basically, if a product has the word *"fresh"* in its name, it's out. If you're doing it right, you will eventually reach a point when you smell like silence, which, as previously mentioned, can be rather unsettling.

Identify the Triggers: This is a moving target. Today's safe scent could be tomorrow's arch-nemesis. Keep a running list of foods, household items, and personal hygiene products that seem to cause a reaction. Then, be prepared to update and discard that list at a moment's notice when everything flip-flops. On a related note, I was forced to dispose of a particularly pungent pair of flip-flops.

Maintain a Safe Zone: Find one room in the house that remains free of all offensive smells. No cooking smells, no scented candles, no strong laundry detergent. Think of it as a neutral zone where she can escape when the world becomes too... fragrant.

Be Ready to Evacuate: You might be enjoying a nice dinner out when suddenly she drops her fork, goes pale, and looks at you with an expression of urgency. At this moment, do not ask questions. Do not hesitate. Simply get up, pay the bill, and execute a swift and silent retreat.

Don't Take It Personally: If she says that you stink, it's not an attack on your hygiene — you're an attack on her nasal passages. The scent of your existence is offensive, that's all. This is temporary *(probably)*, so roll with it.

Pregnancy plays havoc with the senses in ways that defy logic. Your job is to adapt, stay flexible, and, above all, not argue when she sweetly, softly, subtly suggests that you smell like a crime against humanity.

There's More To It

Thus far, we've explored at length how smells alone can trigger a full-scale gastrointestinal rebellion, but that's just the tip of the pregnancy sensory overload iceberg. Smell is merely one sense that can be personally offended. There are others, and they're equally unpredictable.

TASTE: I once prided myself on knowing my wife's food preferences. I could order for her at restaurants with confidence, predict her go-to snacks, and avoid the handful of foods she found unappealing. All of this was useful intel until pregnancy took that knowledge, lit it on fire, laughed as it burned, and tossed the ashes into the wind. Foods she once loved were now personally insulting. Dishes she had detested her entire life suddenly produced cravings so intense they bordered on religious experiences.

Case in point: *sauerkraut*. Historically, she'd treated it with the kind of intense disdain most people reserve for tax audits and clowns. But one night, at a modest little bar and grill, she surprised me by ordering a heaping bowl of the stuff. No sausage, no potatoes. Just fermented cabbage in all its vinegary glory.

She ate it slowly, reverently, eyes closed, wearing the faint, blissed-out smile of someone communing with a higher power. With each forkful, she let out an involuntary sound of pleasure — somewhere between a hum and a low, satisfied moan. It was the kind of noise that, in any other context, might prompt someone to put a sock on the doorknob. I shifted uncomfortably in my seat, glancing around peripherally, and caught the couple at the next table sitting in silence, eyes wide, their forks paused mid-air.

No one said a word, but we were all, I think, quietly agreeing to never speak of it.

SIGHT: It started as an innocent grocery run to procure necessary ingredients for dinner. Tambi was feeling decent, and things were going fine until we reached the meat aisle. That's when I, oblivious to the danger, grabbed a package of chicken.

As I returned to the cart, she must have caught a glimpse of the pink, slippery, raw chicken.

Her body stiffened like an upright cadaver.

A muffled gurgle escaped her throat.

"Put it down," she whispered.

I hesitated.

"PUT IT DOWN", she did not whisper.

I panicked and dropped it into the cart.

I think it was the subtle *"splat"* sound that nudged her over the edge.

In one motion, she turned and bolted for the door. Without hesitation, I abandoned the cart mid-aisle and ran after her. Grocery store employees and fellow shoppers looked on in confusion as we sprinted for the parking lot like fugitives fleeing a crime scene.

When she finally caught her breath, she looked at me, pale but resolute.

"Well," she said, *"I'm done with chicken."*

We had PBJ for dinner.

SOUND: Tambi and I were sitting at the breakfast table. I don't recall what she was eating, but I remember with great clarity that I had just taken a bite of toast.

I was sitting across from her at the breakfast table, minding my own business, when I heard it — the dreaded sharp inhale. I looked up just in time to see her eyes narrow, nostrils flare, and throat convulse.

"Are you... gagging?" I asked, mid-chew.

She quickly raised a hand like a traffic cop.

"Please, stop chewing."

I froze, confused. *"But... I'm just..."*

Her face twisted. *"It's the sound. It's—"* She dry heaved.

Now, I've been accused of many things in my life, but being an offensive chewer has never been one of them. I tested a near-silent nibble, lips sealed like I was harboring political secrets.

"I STILL HEAR IT."

I stared at my toast as if it had betrayed me.

She took a slow, measured breath, trying to calm herself, and then, in a voice filled with both urgency and deep regret, whispered, *"You have to leave."*

And that's the morning I ate toast in the laundry room.

Thankfully, this wasn't a regular occurrence, but it was memorable. The pregnancy nausea came and went, but for some reason, that morning, the sound of me chewing toast was an affront to her earholes. The next day, she happily ate breakfast with me like nothing had happened. But from then on, I've always had a heightened awareness of my mastication volume.

Baby Status Update

Many baby books like to compare fetal size to various fruits or vegetables. A blueberry, a lentil, a kumquat, if they're feeling exotic. But let's try something a little more relatable to the average guy...

By week 8, your baby is now roughly the size of a 10mm socket — that elusive little tool famously known for vanishing from every garage, toolbox, and ratchet set since the dawn of sockets. An appropriate comparison because your tiny baby, like the humble 10mm socket, is indispensable.

While your partner may already be riding a hormonal rollercoaster and sniffing suspiciously at yesterday's favorite foods, remarkable developments are quietly happening within the womb. A tiny, flickering heartbeat begins pulsing away. The brain is forming at high speed. Laying down the foundational structures for memory, emotion, and eventually, the ability to defy any childproof latches you install.

Surreally, none of these new developments are perceptible to Mom. She might be experiencing intense symptoms such as nausea, fatigue, and mood swings, but without any visible confirmation that these significant developments are occurring, it can all seem oddly abstract. Just remember, massive things are happening at a micro-scale. The building blocks of a brand-new person are coming together, cell by microscopic cell.

Action Steps

Be prepared for the swift exit. No warning, no debate — just an impromptu emergency evacuation because the lady with the tuna melt at table three set off a stomach-churning chain reaction. You'll know it's go-time when the nostrils flare, the complexion fades, and the eyes take on that glassy, faraway look. Don't hesitate. Stand up, pay the bill, grab the bags, and relocate her to the nearest patch of breathable air. This particular skill will pay dividends in the future when your offspring decides that the ideal time to fill a Huggies to 150% capacity coincides precisely with the arrival of your entrée.

Stock up on safe foods. Her appetite is now governed by chaos theory. What she devoured yesterday might induce dry-heaving today. Your job is to keep the fridge and pantry stocked with bland, safe, easily digestible food options. Think crackers, plain toast, applesauce, mashed potatoes, oatmeal — basically anything beige and unthreatening. To help with nausea, buy several types of ginger products such as candies, tea, capsules, and ginger ale *(**PRO TIP**: find brands with real ginger, not just flavoring. It's vastly more effective)*. Keep electrolyte drinks like Pedialyte or coconut water on hand for days when she can't keep much else down. Her food preferences may change day-to-day, so don't take it personally if your freshly procured supply of ginger ale is declared to be "*too gingery.*"

Preparing for emotional turbulence. Mood swings aren't just coming — they're probably already parked on the couch in sweatpants. One minute, she's laughing; the next, she's furious that you didn't rinse the spoon before putting it in the dishwasher. Then, just as suddenly, she's hugging you with tears in her eyes because she's *"just so grateful we're doing this together."* It's a lot. But your role here isn't to fix it. Just be calm, present, and patient. Don't try to logic your way through an illogical moment. Just listen, validate, and offer snacks or back rubs as needed. Think of this as emotional boot camp for fatherhood. Your chance to build resilience, compassion, and the ability to stay cool under unpredictable pressure. All of which, by the way, will serve you very well later on.

Create a symptom-tracking system. Set up a simple but effective way to monitor what's happening and when. Use a dedicated notebook or digital tracker *(apps like Ovia or Pregnancy+)* to record daily symptoms, their intensity, time of day, and any triggers or relief methods that worked. This isn't just busy work — it creates valuable data for doctor appointments and helps identify patterns. Track food aversions and cravings, as they tend to change frequently. Note energy levels, emotional fluctuations, and sleep quality. Start recording questions for the doctor as they arise, so nothing gets forgotten. Having this system prevents her from having to mentally catalog everything while feeling terrible, and gives you actionable information to help manage symptoms.

Learning, Adapting, and Becoming Dad

These early months are often some of the most challenging, no doubt about it. You may feel out of your depth. You'll ~~probably~~ definitely mess up. At some point, you may make the regrettable mistake of suggesting that she's being "*a little too sensitive.*" If this happens, fear not; you'll only do this once. The important thing is that you're present, fully engaged, ready to adapt, and making an effort — even if that means eating your breakfast in the quiet company of the washing machine.

BABY SIZE
WEEK 9
"hacky sack"

your legacy

Chapter 3
Weeks 9-13
The Shift

Up until this point, pregnancy had felt a tad... *theoretical*. Sure, I had witnessed my wife endure morning sickness, gag at smells that didn't exist, and cry when she saw a duck. But there was still some part of my brain that just hadn't processed the full gravity of the situation.

Then, we had our first *real* ultrasound appointment.

I say *real* because technically, we'd already had an earlier one, but it didn't exactly blow my mind. There wasn't much to see. The doctor pointed at vague shapes on the screen, and I made the appropriate sounds of acknowledgment while having absolutely no idea what I was looking at.

Today's ultrasound was different. There on the monitor was the shape of a well-formed tiny human, albeit a bit *"gummy-bearish."* There were arms, legs, and a head that seemed to account for 50% of its overall body mass — which, if physical attributes are any guide, probably traces back to my end of the gene pool.

Jokes aside, it was a lot to take in. This was a beautiful moment. Quiet, intimate, and impossibly profound. Before us on the screen, flickering in shades of gray, was the tiny person we had created. A full form. A head, arms, legs, and a gently thumping heart. No longer just an abstract concept or a line on a pregnancy test, but a person. And then, as if sensing my shock, the baby moved.

I turned to Tambi, who was already smiling, clutching my arm, and whispering, "*Oh, Ben, look at our baby!*" And I did. I couldn't look away. As I stood there, engulfed by the weight of the experience, I felt myself getting lighter. A shiver slowly traveled from the top of my head all the way down to the tips of my toes. My fingers felt cold, my lips tingled, and darkness began to creep in from the outer edges of my vision.

I was startled when the technician shook me by the shoulder and gently reminded me to breathe before I passed out. She did so with a familiarity that suggested that I was not the first soon-to-be dad to forget basic biological functions during this particular ultrasound appointment.

Dad's Guide to Not Fainting

Let me walk you through what actually happens at this appointment.

First, there's the waiting room. You'll sit there, flipping through a magazine from 2014 about celebrity baby names, while your wife fills out approximately 47 forms about her medical history. You'll notice other couples in various stages of pregnancy, and you'll try not to stare at the haggard-looking new dad who seems as though he hasn't slept a wink in the last three months.

Then they call you back. The ultrasound room is dimmer than you expect, kind of like a medical movie theater. Your pregnant partner lies down on what looks like a dentist's chair that's been tipped back too far, and you get the awkward little chair next to her. It's now my understanding that the sole purpose of this chair is to reduce the distance between the floor and your skull should you temporarily cease to respirate during the procedure.

The technician will then squirt what looks like blue hair gel on your wife's stomach. They call it *"warming gel,"* but judging by my wife's reaction, their definition of *"warm"* is questionable.

Then comes the moment of truth. The technician starts moving what looks like a TV remote control over your lady's stomach, and suddenly, you see your baby.

All bets are off at this moment. Your brain may short-circuit. One second, you're nodding along like a responsible adult; the next, you're gripping the armrest loudly whispering, *"We made fingers!"* You'll cycle through shock, awe, and terror as the reality of fatherhood lands like an anvil. You might feel the overwhelming urge to high-five the technician. You might cry. If, at any point, your legs start feeling like those of a newborn deer, *please aim away* from the ultrasound machine. They cost upwards of $35,000.

The Shift

If you're anything like me, you may feel something shift within you after this ultrasound. You walk out of the appointment a slightly changed person from when you entered. The world looks a little different. You feel a little different.

Up until now, this whole *"having a baby"* thing has existed primarily in words and abstract concepts. A couple of lines on a pregnancy test. Bouts of morning sickness. A growing list of baby products you're apparently going to need, like blue-tooth-enabled wipe warmers.

But now, you've *seen* them. That tiny, squirmy person with fingers and toes and a beating heart. **Your child.**

And some indescribable thing inside you *changes a little.*

You start noticing details you never paid attention to before. The dad at the grocery store who effortlessly maneuvers a stroller with one hand while wrangling a toddler with the other. The guy at the park hoisting his kid onto his shoulders like it's second nature. You catch yourself wondering: *Will I be that kind of dad?*

You start putting more thought into potential baby names. Suddenly, the name *"Elliot"* makes you pause. *Does that sound like our kid? Would it suit them? What if they grow up to be a scientist? An artist? An athlete? An interpretive dancer?*

You wonder what they'll look like. Will they have your nose? Your partner's eyes? Your left earlobe that hangs ever-so-slightly lower than the right?

And then there are heavier thoughts.

You feel a deep, unspoken responsibility settle squarely onto your shoulders — the knowledge that this tiny, helpless person is going to *need* you. Not just to provide, but to guide, to lead, to inspire, to teach, to protect Someone who earns their trust, who shapes their view of the world, who makes them feel safe.

It's both exhilarating and terrifying.

Because now, more than ever, you *want* to get this right.

When you experience the shift, it's a sign that you're well on your way to becoming the *good dad* that you're meant to be.

Genetic Screening

Typically, around weeks 10-12, your doctor may bring up the topic of genetic screening. If you're like most soon-to-be dads, your immediate reaction will be, *"Wait... why? Is something wrong?"*

Take a breath. The vast majority of the time, these tests are just routine. The purpose of genetic screening is to assess the likelihood of chromosomal conditions like Down syndrome. While these conditions are rare, screening allows doctors to evaluate the odds early on and determine whether further testing is needed.

How Genetic Testing Works

Nobody tells you that genetic testing isn't just one quick test. It's a process. If your partner opts in, here's what to expect:

- **Bloodwork:** A simple blood draw from your partner can analyze fetal DNA circulating in her bloodstream. This is called *noninvasive prenatal testing (NIPT)* and is commonly offered to assess risk for chromosomal abnormalities.
- **Ultrasound measurements:** A *nuchal translucency (NT) scan* is often done between weeks 11-14. This measures the fluid at the back of the baby's neck, which can indicate potential genetic conditions.
- **More bloodwork:** Depending on risk factors and screening results, doctors may order additional tests for a clearer picture.
- **Waiting for results:** This can take anywhere from a few days to two weeks, which will feel like two decades. Avoid

the temptation to go down a Google rabbit hole in the meantime.

Should You Get Genetic Testing?

For most pregnancies, the risk of genetic conditions is very low. Many people opt to skip it altogether. However, testing is often recommended if:

- The mother is 35 or older *(when risks slightly increase)*.
- There's a family history of genetic disorders.
- The doctor identifies any concerns on an ultrasound.

Some parents choose to test for peace of mind, while others prefer not to stress over what *might* happen unless there's a compelling reason to do so. There's no right or wrong decision, but this is an important conversation to have with your partner to determine if it's the right move for you both.

One Bonus Feature

Genetic testing can determine the baby's gender as early as 10 weeks. That said, you'll also have the option to find out at the *mid-pregnancy anatomy ultrasound* around 18-22 weeks. If you do opt for early gender testing, be warned. Once the results are in, an ancient, unstoppable instinct will awaken within your mother-in-law. Almost as if coded into her DNA, she will immediately begin curating nursery color palettes, pre-ordering personalized onesies, and referring to the baby by a name you absolutely did not agree to.

Baby Status Update

At this stage, your baby is roughly the size of a hacky sack. Spherical, dense, and full of potential. A significant improvement from the *"dot of an i"* era, just a couple of months back. But instead of being lobbed about by a circle of guys in cargo pants behind the cafeteria, your kid is gently awash in a protective orb of amniotic fluid.

One of the most notable changes is the development of fingers and toes. The previously webbed little paddles are now separating, which, yes, may hurt their future Olympic swim times — but it's a big win for things like gripping toys, picking their nose, and giving high-fives.

Facial features are also taking shape. Eyes, nose, and mouth are beginning to settle into position, which means you're inching closer to hearing those inevitable and highly subjective declarations like, *"She has your nose!"* or *"He looks just like the UPS driver."*

Reflexes are kicking in, too. Your baby is starting to move its tiny arms and legs, even though your partner won't feel those movements just yet. Muscles and nerves are connecting, and the wee one is beginning to test-drive their new gear.

Internally, things are coming together as well. The liver, kidneys, intestines, and other vital organs are coming online, prepping for their upcoming role of turning milk into, let's just say... memories.

All of these developments are happening fast, and soon enough, your partner will start feeling movement. For now, if she swears she already feels the baby, just nod and go with it. You don't want to die on that hill.

Action Steps

Start researching strollers and cribs. Don't buy them yet, but get familiar with the basics. Read reviews, compare models, and learn the difference between a travel system, a jogging stroller, and whatever that thousand-dollar Scandinavian spaceship is. Yes, you'll fall down a rabbit hole comparing features like *"one-handed fold"* and *"ventilated canopies."* Just know they all essentially do the same thing: roll that baby from point A to point B.

Figure out your parental leave situation. Now may be a good time to have a conversation with HR. Find out what kind of leave you're entitled to — paid, unpaid, or something that technically exists in the employee handbook but no one has actually taken in a decade. If it's unclear, ask questions. If it's flexible, start thinking through how much time you can realistically take off and how to make it work financially. And if your boss is the gatekeeper, now would be a great moment to casually ask about their kids, compliment their tie, and maybe bring them a donut or two.

Make a baby budget. Some baby expenses you can see coming — diapers, wipes, crib, etc. Others will blindside you, like the need for three different types of bottles, a humidifier shaped like a penguin, and a white noise machine that sounds like the outer bands of a hurricane. Start setting aside money now, even if it's just a little each week. Think of it less as a budget and more as a buffer between you and the moment you realize your newborn goes through three outfits, twelve diapers, and 57 wipes a day.

Research and register for childbirth education. Take some time to research options that go beyond standard hospital classes. Consider the Bradley Method, Hypnobirthing, Lamaze, or specialty classes for specific birth plans. Look for curricula that include practical labor support techniques, postpartum preparation, and newborn care — not just breathing exercises or medical interventions. Register for classes scheduled during the second trimester when possible. This is when she'll typically have the most energy and the most time. If in-person options are limited, investigate reputable online programs with good reviews from actual participants.

Start clearing space. Even if the nursery's still a vague concept, now's the time to start reclaiming some square footage. That baby might show up empty-handed, but they'll somehow manage to occupy every room of your home by the end of week one. That guest room closet filled with dusty boxes? It's about to be crammed with diapers, wipes, and backup wipes for the wipes. The living room will become a rotating gallery of swings, loungers, and colorful plastic things that light up and sing at random. Your bathroom cabinet? That'll be dedicated to infant-safe lotion and a baby tub the size of a kayak. Even your nightstand will get overtaken by pacifiers, burp cloths, and a baby monitor.

Make room now. While the to-do list is still short and your weekends are still your own.

THE SECOND TRIMESTER

Welcome to the second trimester — often described as the *"sweet spot"* of pregnancy. Her nausea begins to fade, her energy starts creeping back, and the baby bump finally makes its debut.

People smile more. Strangers offer unsolicited advice. The phrase *"glowing"* gets thrown around a lot, although you may find that glow is mostly a semi-permanent layer of sweat.

Your partner's body is changing fast now — and so is your role. But in the midst of all this, the idea of fatherhood shifts from theoretical to tangible, and you start to understand what it means to be a *good dad*.

This is the trimester where you find your footing. The fog of the first few months begins to lift, and you realize you're not just getting through it anymore — you're actually preparing for something extraordinary.

BABY SIZE
WEEK 14
"your wallet"

pocket-size!

Chapter 4

Weeks 14-17

Enter The Bump

The first time my wife suggested we go on a hike during pregnancy, I was certain she was joking. I'm talking about the type of certainty you have in knowing that the sky is blue, water is wet, and a toddler with a marker is up to no good. I was so certain, in fact, that I applauded her comedic timing right up until the point of realizing that she was lacing up her sneakers.

This was the same person who, just last week, had barely been able to lift her head off the couch without groaning like a senior citizen. The same person who had spent the last few months dry-heaving at the mere mention of *"tuna noodle casserole"* and had been too exhausted to finish a full episode of any show whose title did not explicitly contain the words *"Law & Order."*

And now she wanted to go outside?

In nature?

Voluntarily?

The second trimester had officially arrived, and with it, an entirely new version of my wife. One who had energy again, one who suddenly wanted to go places, and one who, now less frequently, flip-flopped personalities like Jekyll and Hyde.

So, hiking we went. And for the first time, I allowed myself to believe a dangerous thought:

"This pregnancy thing is getting easier!"

I would come to regret that thought when her newfound energy turned into something far more organized and far more dangerous:

A list.

Multi-page, bullet-pointed, and color-coded — covering in extraneous detail everything we needed to accomplish before the baby arrived.

Why It Feels Easier (For Now)

The second trimester is often referred to as the *"Golden Period"* of pregnancy. A brief window where your partner usually feels quite good.

After three months of ups and downs, suddenly, my wife, Tambi, was feeling mostly up. The nausea? Finally backed off. The exhaustion? Less debilitating. The emotions? Still unpredictable, but now with fewer instances of spontaneous sobbing over sightings of puppies, kittens, or ducks.

It's something like waking up after a three-month hangover. One day, your wife emerges from the bathroom without that haunted look in her eyes. She actually finishes breakfast. She suggests going somewhere that isn't the couch or the bathroom. It feels like a miracle. And it kind of is. The hormonal hurricane that ravaged her body and mind during previous months has seemingly dispersed. Her body has adjusted to its new reality. The placenta has taken over hormone production. Biology stuff is happening that basically translates to:

She's back... *sort of.*

This resurgence of energy isn't random. It's nature's way of saying, *"Quick — do everything you can now before I make you too uncomfortable to move again!"* That means projects will begin in earnest. Will they get finished? That's another story entirely. Enthusiasm may be high, but so is something called *"pregnancy brain"*.

One minute, she's reorganizing the pantry. The next, she's hyper-focused on choosing *the* perfect shade of eucalyptus green for the nursery. Then her priorities change to rearranging the living room furniture, only to be distracted by a sudden need to artificially expand the waistband of her Levis with the strategic application of a hairband through the loop and around the button.

Her appetite has returned with a vengeance, and her cravings are no longer cute or casual. They're missions of utmost importance. This isn't *"I could go for some cheese."* This is *"Get me 1/2lb of thin-sliced, imported, smoked gouda from the 3rd Street deli across town, and do not return without it."* The specificity is staggering — as is the cost of failing such a mission.

And let's not forget the curveballs. Foods she loved last week may now be personal insults. Meanwhile, the foods she previously loathed have become the cornerstone of her diet. I once watched my wife devour an entire jar of olives, letting out elongated moans of contentment as if each one were a delectable morsel of tiramisu. This was the same woman who used to refer to olives as — and I quote — *"grape-shaped disappointments."*

So, what the heck is going on here?

It all comes down to hormones and biology. During the second trimester, the body ramps up the production of progesterone and estrogen, which not only helps sustain the pregnancy but also contributes to increased blood flow and metabolism. Hence the surge in energy and appetite. The nesting instinct is an evolutionary trait believed to be a way for expecting mothers to prepare a safe and comfortable environment for their babies.

As for cravings? Scientists aren't entirely sure. This is unfortunate because if you're lady is anything like mine, cravings will keep you on your toes. Some theories suggest that cravings are the body's way of signaling nutritional needs, while others argue it's purely hormonal and sensory. One thing's for sure: *logic does not apply.* Cravings can be unpredictable, urgent, and utterly immune to reason. Your best bet is to accept your role, stay flexible, and keep the car keys within reach.

Enter The Bump

There's a defining moment in every dad-to-be's journey when you stop, look at her, and think:

"Holy crap. There really is a person growing in that belly."

For me, that moment came one random evening when my wife's belly walked into the room, followed shortly thereafter by my wife.

I'm not talking about just a little after-dinner belly. Not just a weird angle or strange lighting. A real, undeniable, round, baby-containing belly. I stared at her obviously protruding stomach as if I was seeing it for the first time. In this particular way, I was.

"*Whoa,*" I muttered under my breath.

Judging by the way she whipped around and focused her attention squarely upon me, she must have heard my inadvertent commentary in regard to her increasingly shapely lower frontal region.

Our eyes met. Mine widened. Her's narrowed. We stared at each other for a few seconds. Neither of us spoke. Then she smiled with a smirk and sat down next to me on the sofa.

It wasn't that I didn't believe the baby was there. I had seen the ultrasounds. I had experienced, second-hand, the drastic changes her body was going through. But this was different. This was undeniable. An entirely new level of *real*.

Then, just as I was wrapping my head around this, she grabbed my hand and pressed it against her belly.

"*Feel it?!?*

I froze, unsure of the context. Was that a question or a statement? Was she referring to the rotund, plumpness of her midsection? Years of marital experience had taught me that I needed to choose my words carefully.

But then I was spared.

The baby kicked!

I involuntarily jerked my hand away like I had touched a hot stove.

Another undeniable piece of evidence that there was a living thing in there. A moving, kicking, living thing.

And just like that, yet another entirely fresh wave of shock and awe washed over me.

Unsolicited Touching

The baby bump is officially making its debut, and with it comes the jarring new experience of unsolicited belly-touching.

The first time it happened to us was in the cereal aisle. A middle-aged woman, who was a stranger to us both, walked up, placed both hands on my wife's stomach, and said, *"Definitely a boy!"*

I stood there frozen, Fruity Pebbles in hand, watching my wife's face rapidly cycle through a broad range of emotions before settling on forced politeness. Thankfully, she didn't land on the emotion of *uninhibited wrath* because the woman would have been vaporized where she stood, leaving behind only a pair of smoldering one-inch heels as the only evidence of her prior existence.

The interesting thing is that this wasn't an isolated incident. Suddenly, my wife's body had become public property. Coworkers would comment on her size. Family members would touch her without warning. Even my buddy Eric, who normally wouldn't notice if you shaved your eyebrows off, became so fixated that he would regularly remark, *"I can't stop looking at it!"*

Each time someone took a special interest in her belly, I observed Tambi's smile get a little tighter, a little more forced.

Realizing that I had to intervene, I took on the unexpected role of *"The Belly Buffer"* — strategically positioning myself between my wife and potential touchers, ready to intercept wandering hands with a friendly but firm, "*She's not comfortable with belly touching.*" This strategy works about 70% of the time. The other 30%, my wife handles herself in ways that make me simultaneously impressed and terrified.

The Secret Is Out

The baby bump is a milestone. It's the moment when pregnancy transitions from assumption to undeniable reality. But the unsolicited touching isn't the only thing that comes with the baby bump. It also changes how the world sees her.

Before the bump, pregnancy was invisible. A secret.

But now? *The secret is out.*

Strangers smile at her in public. Little old ladies strike up conversations about motherhood. Cashiers ask if it's her first baby. Cashiers also ask if I'm the father. Every trip outside turns into a miniature social event where well-meaning people offer advice, ask about baby names, and regale her with unsolicited labor stories that nobody asked for.

And while most of it is sweet and well-intended, it can also be exhausting or even irritating.

So here's your job, dear reader:

- **Be her escape plan:** If someone corners her with a 15-minute dissertation concerning the advantages of cloth diapers, have an excuse on standby. *"Oh, wow, we better get going — I think we left the oven on in the car."*

- **Run interference:** If you see someone approaching with *that look* — the one that says, *"Imma touch dat belly"* — step in. Recall an urgent appointment elsewhere. Fake a heart attack. Do *something*.
- **Validate her feelings:** If she's thrilled that people are excited, celebrate with her. If she's over it and just wants to get through Target without a single human interaction, support that, too.

While the baby bump is a beautiful milestone, it can also be quite the public spectacle. She's going to need you in her corner.

Stretchy Pants

One day, her jeans fit just fine. The next, her waistband has declared war on her lower abdomen. That's when you realize you're about to embark on yet another crucial mission in your journey as an expectant dad: helping her choose stretchy pants that will accommodate a rapidly swelling uterus and an ever-expanding sense of discomfort.

Most men have accumulated some level of experience in the fine art of helping their lady shop for jeans. You might even consider yourself a seasoned veteran, having stood outside the fitting room, holding six nearly identical pairs, nodding with approval when she asks, *"How does my butt look in these?"* Maybe you've fetched alternate sizes, weighed in on pocket placement, or dared to utter an opinion on wash or cut. If so, congratulations. You've been through the minor leagues. Maternity pants, however, are on another level entirely. This is no longer about that button-fly, butt-lifting, stone-wash nonsense. This is about structural integrity.

48

The big difference is that *"pants,"* in the traditional sense, are designed to accommodate the lower half of a single human. *"Maternity pants,"* however, are a marvel of modern engineering, with the unique purpose of dressing *one-and-a-half* humans. What makes this feat possible is a highly stretchy fabric called *elastic*, developed originally to catch F18 Hornets making an emergency landing on aircraft carriers, which has now been repurposed to keep maternity pants in place when traditional denim waves the white flag.

I spent an entire Saturday moving from store to store, standing patiently beside racks of maternity wear while holding my wife's purse like the dutiful husband I am. Each pair of pants she tried on came with its own unique *"belly band architecture,"* and my role was to observe, ask discerning questions like *"Is that more of an over-the-bump or under-the-bump situation?"* and pretend I understood the difference between a cotton blend and lyocell knit. By the end, I had developed passionate opinions on stretch recovery and panel width, and we walked away from the store with two fresh pairs of maternity pants in the shopping bag.

It's usually early in the second trimester when her body begins to change visibly, and stretchy pants are just the first in a long line of wardrobe replacements. The Southern end of her shirts will begin creeping North. Bras will strain to accommodate their increasingly voluminous payload. Shoes will mysteriously shrink by two sizes overnight. And while she's the one carrying the weight of these changes — *both literally and figuratively* — these changes belong to both of you.

Your role is to stand by with gentle eyes and steady hands as she cycles through garment after garment, helping her build an ever-evolving rotation of clothing capable of rising to the noble task of containing her increasingly miraculous shape. You'll exude patience. You will hold hangers. You will offer honest, tactful feedback that walks the impossible tightrope between support and survival. And you'll mean it, because while there are elements of comedy laced into every facet of this process, watching her become a woman who will ultimately bring new life into this world is one of the most humbling, beautiful, and awe-inspiring parts of the whole journey.

Lessons Learned

Just because she has energy doesn't mean she's not exhausted. Pregnancy is still draining. Even if she's up and moving around more, she still needs rest. I learned this after my wife spent an entire Sunday reorganizing our pantry storage spaces and then crashed so hard that she couldn't get out of bed until Tuesday. Her energy comes in waves now. Intense productivity followed by equally intense fatigue. Your job is to recognize when she's pushing too hard and try to gently throttle her enthusiasm.

Mood swings aren't gone either; they're just sneakier. One moment, she's joking about her belly getting bigger. Next, she's crying because her belly is getting bigger. Adapt accordingly. The emotional rollercoaster of the second trimester might have gentler dips, but it's still very much a rollercoaster.

Now is one of those times where it pays to put a tad more effort into anticipating her needs. She has a multitude of things on her mind. The more you can do without being asked, the better. The mental load of pregnancy is enormous. Your wife isn't just growing a human; she's planning for a complete life transformation. Share some of that load. Help her process her thoughts, feelings, and emotions.

Baby Status Update

At this stage, your baby is roughly the size of your wallet, which feels oddly appropriate. While they're growing bigger by the week, your wallet may be experiencing the opposite effect as you stock up on diapers, baby gear, nursery items, and enough wipes to wipe the collective posteriors of a well-stocked zoo. It's a poetic little preview of fatherhood, if you think about it. You're wallet gets smaller, they get bigger — and yet, I can promise you that you'll eventually acknowledge that it's still the best deal you've ever made.

Additionally, your baby can now frown, squint, yawn, and even suck its thumb. It's both a bizarre and adorable realization that your baby is already showing little signs of personality while floating around in amniotic fluid. You can't see it, but one minute, they're peacefully sleeping; the next, they're practicing their best impression of your mother-in-law's disapproving glare — all before they've even seen daylight.

The skeleton is hardening, and muscles are strengthening, meaning kicks are starting to become more apparent. Your partner isn't imagining it anymore. Around now is when you can begin to feel kicks from the outside, a sensation not unlike having someone gently tap a water balloon from the inside — equal parts miraculous and unsettling. The first time you feel it, you'll likely yank your hand away in shock as if you've accidentally touched a live wire, and then immediately press it back, hoping for an encore.

Your baby can hear sounds now, which means you can start talking to them. Feel awkward talking to a belly? You'll get over it. This is merely the first in a long series of dignity-sacrificing moments that fatherhood will require of you. Your baby is already learning to recognize voices, including yours. I started reading aloud whatever book I happened to be into at the time, which is how our unborn child became intimately familiar with the geopolitical tensions of Middle-earth, the eating habits of hobbits, and the long-term psychological toll of carrying a cursed ring across hostile terrain.

Action Steps

Be the belly buffer. Your partner is now sporting undeniable evidence of your collective life choices. Apparently, this is an open invitation for every stranger within a three-mile radius to reach out and touch. Develop a strategy — whether it's the subtle sidestep, the casual conversation redirection, or the more direct *"back-off, weirdo!"* statement delivered with a smile. Practice makes perfect, and you'll need this skill for approximately the next five months.

Be the midnight snack sherpa. The second trimester cravings aren't just suggestions — they're biological imperatives. When she sits bolt upright at 2 AM and announces that she needs a peanut butter and pickle sandwich, your response shall not be *"Really? Now?"* Instead, it's *"Crunchy or smooth?"* Keep the pantry stocked, know which 24-hour stores have the good ice cream, and consider setting up a dedicated shelf for her current rotation of must-haves. Future You will thank Present You when you're not driving across town at midnight.

Take advantage of the Golden Period. The second trimester energy surge won't last forever. Use this time to tackle more significant projects that will be much harder to complete later —

whether that's assembling furniture, taking a babymoon vacation, or finally fixing that wonky shelf that's been bothering her since 2019. Remember, the third trimester will bring its own unique challenges, not the least of which is that your partner will struggle to put on her socks. Make the most of this fleeting time to get essential things done.

BABY SIZE
WEEK 18
"can of beer"

Cheers!
You made this!

Chapter 5
Weeks 18-21
Blue or Pink?

The anatomy scan, typically done between 18 and 22 weeks, is a deep dive into your baby's development. It's not just a check-up — it's *the* check-up. They confirm organs, estimate the due date, verify that everything is on track, and even tell you the sex of your baby... *if you're ready to know.*

When we walked into the appointment, I felt a wild mix of emotions — excitement, nerves, and a general feeling of uneasiness that often accompanies those who are about to learn something potentially life-changing.

Minutes later, an image popped up on the screen. Ever since the last ultrasound, I had mentally associated our baby with the general likeness of a gummy bear. That was no longer the case. There, on the screen before us, clear as day, was a tiny, fully formed human being. Moving, stretching, and, as I was about to learn, plotting a surprise attack.

Everything was going smoothly. The tech was scanning, sliding the probe to various positions on my wife's slippery belly, taking measurements, and explaining different body parts. Then, mid-scan, our in-utero child decided they were done with the paparazzi.

A swift, forceful, upwards kick occurred. This well-executed strike landed with precision directly into the probe that was resting on my wife's belly. It felt like a moment straight out of a slapstick comedy. The ultrasound probe recoiled from the blow, causing the image on the screen to distort. The technician blinked. My wife gasped. I nodded in silent approval.

"Wow," the tech said, repositioning the equipment. *"That was a strong one."*

My brain immediately fast-forwarded to the future athletic possibilities this might suggest. Soccer? Karate? MMA?

Once the tech had regained control of the situation, the appointment continued without further violence.

The Gender

It's often during this particular appointment that you will be given the option to learn whether you'll soon become the proud father of a boy or a girl.

Are you ready to find out?

For some, the answer is easy: *"Yes, tell us! We need to know!"* For others, the answer is an equally easy *"No."* And then there's the middle ground; when one of you wants to know now, the other prefers to wait, in which case no small degree of careful negotiations may ensue.

Regardless of what you choose, you'll be finding out eventually, and when you do, just be prepared that there will be an onslaught of opinions coming your way.

"Were you hoping for a boy or a girl?"

"We waited and were surprised — <u>it was the best</u>!"

"Ultrasounds aren't always accurate, you know."

We were firmly in the *"tell us now"* camp, and we communicated this to the ultrasound tech. As we stared at the screen, they took a deep breath, smiled at us, and said three little words:

"It's a girl."

A whirlwind of emotions hit me all at once. Excitement. Wonder. A heavy sense of reality sank in even further.

This was no longer just *a baby*.

This was my daughter.

2D, 3D, 4D

Ultrasounds come in three distinct flavors: 2D, 3D, and 4D — each offering a slightly different sneak peek at your baby.

2D ultrasounds are the classic, black-and-white images. The ones doctors need, and also the ones that are most helpful from a purely medical perspective. They measure growth, check for abnormalities, and confirm that everything is on track. They're a bit like an old-school video game. Functional, but not exactly lifelike.

3D ultrasounds offer enhanced detail. Instead of vague shadows, you get something closer to a real baby face. You might see chubby cheeks, a little button nose, or a mysteriously furrowed brow. Sometimes, they'll depict the baby as being adorable. Other times, they may look more like a sentient yam. Either way, rest assured that you're baby will look much better in the light of day.

4D ultrasounds add the dimension of movement, so you can watch your baby stretching, yawning, or engaging in liquid-suspended break-dancing in real-time. It's a little like watching a live feed from the world's smallest submarine passenger. Some parents find it profoundly moving. Others find it somewhat eerie. Both are right.

So, which one should you go for? 2D is the standard and necessary. 3D and 4D are optional, primarily for parents who just can't wait to see their baby's face. Some find them magical. Others find them unsettling. If you do opt for one, just remember: you're not seeing the final draft — more like a low-light sneak preview from inside the world's weirdest photo booth.

The Gender Reveal?

Once you know your baby's gender, you'll be faced with a question:

Are you doing a gender reveal — and if so — how dramatic are you going to get?

You may already be aware of this trend, but gender reveals have spiraled wildly out of control. What began as a simple *slice-into-a-colored-cake moment* has transformed into a full-blown arms race of pyrotechnics, aerial stunts, and environmental hazards.

I've seen exploding balloons, bonfires, smoke cannons, drone formations, and one particularly ambitious couple who used an alligator to bite into a colored watermelon.

And then, of course, there are the stunts gone wrong. The car burnout that began in the cul-de-sac and ended in the neighbor's living room. The helicopter confetti drop that resulted in a lawsuit. The gender reveal baseball, filled with appropriately colored powder, that Grandpa hit squarely with the bat, but the ball did not burst until it impacted dear Aunt Susan in the face at a high rate of speed.

All quite memorable occasions, I must admit.

Here's my take on all of this...

If your gender reveal requires the use of a fire department permit, insurance policy, lawyer on retainer, or an emergency evacuation plan — perhaps it's time to reevaluate your priorities.

Our Gender Reveal

We went in the complete opposite direction of many. Low drama, no cameras, minimal fanfare.

We procured a pair of pink baby slippers, visited my parents, sat down casually, and at a completely random moment in the conversation, without a word of context, we handed them a single pink slipper.

They held it, blinked, processed the scarce information before them, and then the message suddenly became clear. Their faces lit up like I'd never seen before. My mom gasped, my dad grinned ear to ear, and the room instantly overflowed with pure joy.

Simple. Intimate. Beautiful.

The Name Game

Now that you *(probably)* know the baby's sex, you've officially unlocked a new phase of preparation: *choosing a name.*

This is a big one.

You may assume this will be a fun and casual conversation. It is not. Instead, this is a high-stakes negotiation filled with immediate vetoes, knee-jerk decisions based on deep-seated grudges, and an alarming number of irrational deal-breakers. You are about to discover that both yourself and your partner, whether you realized it prior or not, have ironclad blacklists of names that can never, under any circumstances, be used.

Here are some ways that the conversation may flow:

You suggest a seemingly reasonable name, and she responds with...

"No. That was the name of a girl in second grade who stole my markers."

"Absolutely not. That's my ex's cousin's brother's dog's name."

"I worked with a guy named that. He drank hot dog water."

Next, she responds with her idea of a suitable baby name, to which you reply...

"Isn't that the name of a medieval torture device?"

"I don't think I can name my child after an herb."

"That sounds like someone who gets paid in singles."

Eventually, you'll reach a point in the back-and-forth name search when all potential names will sound weird, perhaps even your own. You'll spend hours scrolling through endless name lists, rejecting names before even saying them out loud. You'll experiment with different styles — classic, modern, vintage, edgy — only to realize that nothing sounds quite right.

And then, one night, while brushing your teeth or staring into the fridge, one of you will randomly throw out a name, and it kinda works. Over time, you'll accumulate several contenders, and you'll begin testing them in real-world scenarios.

You might not realize it, but names have to pass a series of practical tests, such as:

The POTUS Test: *"Ladies and gentlemen, the President of the United States, [baby's name]!"* You never know.

The Playground Test: Does this name rhyme with anything terrible? If it does, the mean kids will find it in a matter of minutes and exploit it to devastating effect. This explains why the Mitches, Barts, and Tuckers of the world often possess heightened levels of resilience.

The Anger Test: *"[Baby's name], get down from the roof!"*

The Initials Test: Do the initials spell out anything unfortunate? M.T.V.? P.M.S.? A young schoolmate of mine was named Andrew Savoy Smith. He became a proctologist.

In the end, you'll find the name that just feels right. It might take weeks or months, but when you do, you'll know. And when you finally say it aloud when looking into the eyes of your child — it's almost as if they've had that name the whole time, and you just needed to discover it.

By the way, if you need some help in choosing a suitable baby name, might I suggest that *Benjamin* is a good, strong choice for a boy, or perhaps the more feminine *Benjamina* for a little lady?

Sex During Pregnancy?

Ah, yes — the topic you've been quietly anticipating since page one. I do hope that my delaying of this particular topic until this point in the book has not been the cause of a multi-month stretch of monk-like abstinence.

The simple answer to the question is: *YES*, you can still have sex during pregnancy. In fact, for most of it, it's not only allowed — it's perfectly healthy, safe, and even encouraged.

Some guys, either out of fear or misinformed chivalry, mistakingly assume that pregnancy is a complete and total moratorium on all bedroom activity. *"I didn't want to poke the baby,"* they'll say in a tone reserved for those recounting acts of great valor. A noble sentiment to be sure, but allow me to gently offer an alternative perspective...

Even if you happen to be as well-endowed as Seabiscuit, there's no degree of coitus — vigorous, acrobatic, celebratory, or otherwise — that would result in the baby being poked. The baby is safely afloat within a fortified, fluid-filled pod, located *well above* your area of operations. So rest easy, champ. If you're still nervous, the OB-GYN will gladly confirm this for you with a hardly-noticeable smirk if you dare to ask.

Now, is sex different during pregnancy? Absolutely. One of the most influential factors is that her hormones are doing all sorts of wacky things, which can have a direct and unpredictable effect on her libido. This causes some pregnant women to become walking romance novels — glowing, swooning, and suddenly interested in exploring levels of physical affection typically reserved for honeymoon suites and cable TV after 11 p.m. Others experience a full-body shutdown, resulting in a period of devout celibacy, flannel pajamas, and an allergic reaction to touch.

In my case, Tambi cycled through both extremes. One day, she would issue a stern no-touch policy banning all forms of physical contact, including the inadvertent brushing of knees on the couch. The next day, she'd look at me like a ravenous lioness stalking an all-you-can-eat-man-meat buffet — and then pounce with such unbridled enthusiasm that I'd find myself wondering afterwards if we had just conceived another baby or three.

As pregnancy progresses and her belly begins to defy gravity and spatial reasoning, you'll find that intimacy may require a few key adjustments. Think of it as a gentle departure from your standard bedroom choreography and an enthusiastic embrace of The Kama Sutra: Pregnancy Edition. You'll become acquainted with moves like *The Supported Side Snuggle, The Over-The-Bump, Bump,* and the ever-popular *Reverse Pillow Fort.* I did consider providing detailed illustrations for reference purposes, but my graphic designer threatened to walk if I insisted. Suffice it to say that the goal here isn't acrobatics. It's comfort, connection, and working around the new geography of her magnificent, ever-expanding baby belly. Be gentle. Be patient. Be ready to laugh when things go sideways. If all else fails, that's why God invented spooning.

Sometimes it just turns out that intimacy isn't in the cards for a stretch of time. If this happens, remember that closeness isn't just about sex. Cuddling, back rubs, foot rubs, forehead kisses, doing the dishes without being asked — all of these acts of love count in a big way. This is a time to build intimacy in all its forms, even if not necessarily the one you were hoping for.

Finally, if you're still nervous, talk to your doctor together. There are some situations where sex may be temporarily off the table, such as certain complications, high-risk pregnancies, or instructions to rest. But in a healthy, low-risk pregnancy, you're generally in the clear to go for it.

Baby Status Update

At this stage, your baby is roughly the size and weight of a can of beer. Yes, I've just likened your precious offspring to a chilled brewski — a comparison I'm confident no other pregnancy book would dare make. One is a comforting beverage to enjoy at the end of a long day. The other is a rapidly growing source of discomfort, currently rearranging your partner's organs and emotions. One day soon, you'll be holding that little human in your arms, and not even a foamy cold one will bring you more comfort than that. While I'll do my best to avoid comparing your in utero baby to a box of pinot grigio in a later chapter, I make no firm promises.

They're also becoming more intricate, more detailed, more human. Facial features are fine-tuning, limbs are lengthening, and their tiny fingers and toes are now fully formed. This is also when the baby starts practicing facial expressions. Their ears are fully developed, meaning they can hear sounds from the outside world. The combination of these two developments means that if you've begun practicing your dad jokes, there's a chance they may already be rolling their eyes.

This is also the time when the baby's movements become far more noticeable. Those first little flutters? They're turning into more distinct jabs, rolls, and stretches. All of these new movements are your baby's way of testing out their ever-strengthening muscles.

Some studies suggest that babies can be soothed by familiar sounds. I took this as my cue to start shaping our child's impeccable taste in music by playing a carefully curated mix of jazz and classic rock.

Did the baby approve? Hard to say, but based on the rhythmic belly thumps, they definitely had strong preferences. A mellow sway during Miles Davis, but the second AC/DC blasted through the speaker? Wild, untamed kicks. We couldn't decide if she was jamming along or trying to escape the womb. Either way, I chose to believe I was doing my part to raise a tiny rock-and-roll aficionado with a deep appreciation for face-melting lead guitar solos.

Action Steps

Prep for the anatomy scan while avoiding Dr. Google. The big ultrasound is approaching, and while it's tempting to research every possible outcome, limit yourself to understanding the basics. Know what they're checking for without memorizing a medical textbook's worth of potential abnormalities. Your job is to be present, hold her hand, and refrain from asking the technician if they can check whether the baby has your nose while they're trying to measure critical organs.

Keep your priorities straight regarding gender. Whether you're hearing the news in a quiet ultrasound room or amid a cloud of confetti, it's easy to get swept up in the spectacle. But remember what actually matters: *a healthy baby and a healthy mama*. That's the win. Boy or girl is just a detail. While it's natural to have preferences or daydreams, this isn't about getting your wish. It's about meeting whoever this little person turns out to be. The goal isn't pink or blue. It's gratitude. Keep your heart tuned to that, and however the announcement goes down, you'll be exactly where you need to be.

Start early and keep a name list. Maybe she's always wanted to honor her grandfather. Perhaps you still have unresolved trauma with a kid named *"Bradley"* who pantsed you in gym class. Maybe she's genuinely interested in the name *"Salvadore Moonbeam,"* while you're thinking something more along the lines of *"Dave."* These are all important details to consider and record. Approach the process with curiosity and openness. To keep things organized, create a shared note or spreadsheet where you can both jot down ideas as they come. Include a section for vetoed names as well. The name list will save you from the inevitable moment where one of you says, *"What was that name we both liked last week?"* and the other stares into the void. The list will probably grow to dozens — perhaps hundreds — before you eventually circle back to one of the first five. That's part of the process.

BABY SIZE
WEEK 22
"3 donuts"

Baking in progress!

Chapter 6

Weeks 22-26

Thermostat Roulette

As a man in a long-term relationship with a woman, I've learned that verbal communication is an art form. One with a steep learning curve and real-time consequences. And now, with pregnancy in full swing, the stakes have risen dramatically.

Parts of her anatomy are rapidly expanding. Hormones are conducting experiments on exciting new emotional combinations. Her self-image is becoming more fragile by the hour. And into this highly flammable atmosphere strolls you, holding a metaphorical sparkler.

The danger is that pregnancy introduces a growing list of observations you will be tempted to comment on — and an even longer list of reasons you should abstain from doing so.

Yes, she cried over a dish detergent commercial.

Yes, she peed a little bit when she sneezed.

Yes, she's sweating in a room set to 63 degrees.

Yes, she fell asleep at 4:30 p.m. while holding a fork.

Yes, her bra is well beyond its intended load-bearing capacity.

This volatile environment means that while your observations may be factually accurate, this does not give you the liberty to orate such opinions without careful consideration. To be perfectly direct, under no circumstances should comparisons be made between various parts of her anatomy and large fruits, hot-air balloons, or celestial bodies.

One example I can provide is of a seemingly innocuous phrase I once muttered, but came to regret approximately 1 millisecond after the words departed my lips:

"Are we certain there's just one baby in there?"

...

...

...

As you can imagine, this was a mistake. The fact that you're reading my words means that I was not vaporized. However, justice for my transgression was swift and severe. I was immediately sentenced to a lengthy stretch of cold-shouldered silence and an emotional purgatory that made even our dog avoid eye contact with me. For several days, I lived as a man on the fringe — not quite exiled, but certainly not welcome in polite conversation. I became unusually familiar with the quiet rhythms of household chores and the subtle language of sighs. My penance included countless foot rubs, acts of service bordering on bribery, and a standing offer to procure any snack she desired, regardless of rarity or distance. Eventually, I was allowed to re-enter her good graces after proving myself within a period of probation.

Suffice it to say that words are far more than just breathy noises leaving your mouth. They have great power, and with great power comes great responsibility. Words can lift her up, reassure her, and remind her that she is strong, beautiful, and capable, even when she's feeling exhausted and unsure. On the contrary, words also have the power to inadvertently cause your domicile to become restricted to the couch for the foreseeable future.

Examples of good commentary:

"You're absolutely glowing, honey."

"This pregnancy thing really suits you."

"You're becoming more beautiful every day."

Examples of bad commentary:

"I think your belly entered the room before you did."

"Did that shirt shrink in the wash?"

"You have HOW many months left?"

The line between compliment and insult will become increasingly blurry over the next few months, so when in doubt, err on the side of flattery, admiration, and unwavering support. A helpful litmus test may be that if you wouldn't say it to a pregnant, hormonal, sleep-deprived mama grizzly bear, it's likely best to avoid saying it to your partner.

Sleep Schedule Shenannigans

It was around this time that I noticed my wife's sleep schedule was beginning to lose any form of repeatability, structure, or logic.

To preface this, you should know that my Tambi is usually the kind of person who stays up quite late, sleeps like a log through the night, and then awakens in a slow-burning funk that is gradually extinguished with a liberal application of coffee. This is her normal. She is not, nor has she ever been, a morning person. I had come to accept this as an irrefutable law of nature.

Hence my astonishment when I was awoken at 4 AM to find her deep-cleaning the kitchen. Other nights, she'd be up until dawn researching strollers like she was writing a doctoral dissertation. On more than a few days, she'd sleep in well past noon and then approach me with a simple, but urgent request:

"*I want waffles.*"

I tried keeping track of her sleep patterns, but this turned out to be an exercise in futility.

"*So, you went to bed at 9 PM last night, woke up at 2 AM for an hour, then slept until 7 AM. Maybe tonight will be roughly the same?*"

Nope. She stayed up most of the night, crashed at 5 AM, woke up at 3 PM, and once again wanted waffles.

Feeling unsure about how to support her during this particularly odd stage, I turned to one of the pregnancy books I had been referencing. It offered the following kernel of knowledge:

"*Alterations in circadian rhythm, sleep architecture, and overall sleep homeostasis are common physiological responses during pregnancy, largely driven by fluctuations in reproductive hormones such as progesterone, estrogen, and human chorionic gonadotropin (hCG). These hormonal shifts can disrupt REM cycles, increase nighttime awakenings, and contribute to fragmented or non-restorative sleep, particularly as the pregnancy progresses into later stages."*

This translates roughly to, "*You're screwed, buddy.*"

I resigned myself to the reality that predictability was no longer part of our lives. Trying to establish a routine was as pointless as trying to guess which food she'd love or hate on any given day, although waffles had become a reliable dietary staple as of late.

Eventually, I stopped questioning it. If she were up, I'd make her tea. If she needed a snack, I'd pop Eggos in the toaster. If she crashed in the middle of the day, I'd do my best to keep things quiet. Besides, if pregnancy was already this unpredictable, I had a feeling newborn sleep schedules weren't going to be any more forgiving. The best move, I figured, was to roll with it.

Thermostat Roulette

Not only had Tambi's sleep schedule gone off the rails, but her internal thermostat was also acting up — fluctuating with chaotic unpredictability and with no regard for actual external temperatures.

One minute, she'd be huddled under blankets, shivering like she was braving a snowstorm in the Yukon. The next, she'd erupt from her cocoon like a sweaty butterfly, tossing the covers, kicking away pillows, and fanning herself with anything within reach, while declaring with great drama, *"Why is it **so effin' hot** in here?"* Meanwhile, I, an ordinary non-gestating male experiencing what most would refer to as *"room temperature"*, would sit and observe her unusual behavior in confusion. This wasn't a one-time event. It wasn't even a phase. It became a defining feature of our existence.

To help her be more comfortable, we began making regular adjustments to the thermostat. Eventually, these adjustments evolved into a full-blown domestic game I started referring to as *thermostat roulette*. Each night, the dial swung wildly between desert inferno and polar expedition, depending on how her body temperature was behaving at the time. The irony, of course, is that this system worked rather well — *for her*. She was more comfortable, more rested, and blissfully unaware that I had become a climate refugee in my own home. I learned to endure the extremes. One night, I'd be lying atop the covers, nearly nude, with a me-shaped sweat outline beneath me. The next, I'd be burrowed under a mound of blankets as the room's temperature dipped to meat-locker levels.

So what in the frozen heck is going on here?

Her body is working overtime. Blood volume is increasing dramatically, her metabolism is cranked up like a space heater on steroids, and hormone levels are fluctuating faster than the crypto market. Progesterone, in particular, is notorious for messing with the hypothalamus *(the part of the brain that controls body temperature)*, turning it into a bipolar temperature regulator. One moment, she's overheating, and the next, blood flow is rerouting itself in creative ways, leaving her limbs cold and her nose frozen.

There is no predicting where she'll land on the temperature spectrum from one minute to the next. You might walk into the room and find her bundled up like a hiker attempting an Everest summit. Return five minutes later, and she's sprawled out, dramatically misting her sweat-speckled body with a spray bottle.

Your best bet? Don't fight it. Don't question it. Just keep a blanket within arm's reach, stash a fan on her side of the bed, and maybe invest in one of those neck-cooling towels that athletes use. These things won't directly fix anything, but they'll go a long way toward helping her be as comfortable as possible.

If you're feeling confused, just remember: *she is too.*

Only hotter.

Or colder.

Probably both.

Getting Emotional

Somewhere around the halfway point of pregnancy, something strange starts to happen. You — *yes, you* — begin to feel things. Real things. Emotional things. You catch yourself casually talking to the bump. You feel a sudden, irrational urge to karate-chop a stranger who lights a cigarette too close to your wife. And one day, you'll be standing in a store holding some tiny, adorable baby product, and boom — *it hits you.*

For me, it was a pink baby cardigan. We were casually walking through the baby aisle when I saw it: soft, knitted, with little wooden buttons and a hood with lace trim. It fit in the palm of my hand. At that moment, my brain constructed a series of visuals. I pictured my infant daughter cradled in my arms, nursing from a bottle — then toddling down a sidewalk, clutching my finger — then she was a little older, running ahead of me at the park, pigtails bouncing — then I saw her in a Halloween costume, climbing into my lap with sticky fingers — then she was a teenager, rolling her eyes at my jokes but still letting me hug her when no one was watching — then somehow, impossibly, she was grown, waving goodbye from a car window.

I stood there motionless, the little pink cardigan in hand, misty-eyed and emotional like a male actor from a Hallmark movie. Tambi noticed. She didn't say anything right away. She just smiled, walked over, wrapped her arm around mine, and whispered, *"I know."*

And that's when it truly clicks. While she's growing the baby on the inside, you're growing into something just as important — a *good dad*.

Baby Status Update

Picture a single donut lying flat on the table. Now, carefully stack two more on top. You're now looking at a tower of three delectable donuts, which, surprisingly, is roughly the current size of your baby. Now, a word of caution — under no circumstances should you mention this comparison out loud. Even whispering the word *"donut"* within a three-room radius of your pregnant partner carries a 137% chance of triggering a craving so intense, you'll be immediately dispatched to the nearest Dunkin.

Another significant development is *(drumroll)* fingerprints! They can also yawn *(adorable)* and stretch *(understandable)*. If your partner starts feeling a consistent, rhythmic twitching sensation in her belly, it's probably not the baby practicing Morse code — it's hiccups. Totally normal.

Inside, your baby's lungs are developing rapidly in preparation for that first breath of air. Their facial features are becoming more distinct. Their skin is still translucent, but beginning to thicken. They're gaining weight, storing fat, and starting to look less like a tiny potato and more like a small, squishy person. At around 1.5 to 2 pounds and 12–14 inches long, they're roughly the size of a spaghetti squash, though much cuter and eventually far more opinionated.

Your baby is growing fast, reacting to the world, and becoming a little person with their rhythms, quirks, and personality. Keep talking to them. Keep marveling at the weirdness and wonder of it all. You're getting closer to meeting this tiny human. The craziest part? They're already getting to know you.

Action Steps

Develop a compliment repertoire. Generic *"you look great"* platitudes won't cut it anymore. Get creative and specific with your praise: *"Your hair is extra shiny today,"* or *"That color really brings out your eyes."* The more detailed and sincere the compliment, the less likely it'll be mistaken for some clumsy attempt to downplay the noticeable changes she's going through. And while there's a strange societal notion that a round female body isn't attractive, the truth is there are few things more extraordinary, more powerful, or more flat-out beautiful than the female body doing its magic to bring another life into this world. Have some perspective. Let her know she's gorgeous. Not just because it's the right thing to say, but because it's the truth.

Create a flexible sleep support system. This one is tricky. I can generally advise that you need to be prepared for anything. Stock the kitchen with easy midnight snacks. Keep a selection of pillows within arm's reach. Master the art of making waffles at 3 AM without appearing the least bit inconvenienced. Your ability to cheerfully accommodate her bizarre new circadian rhythm will directly correlate to your standing as a competent life partner. You'll get the hang of what she requires to be as well-rested as possible... and then it'll inevitably change. That's the way it goes.

Lean into your emerging dad emotions. You might not have expected it, but at some point, you're going to get misty-eyed over something completely ridiculous — like a pair of impossibly small baby socks, or a scene in a movie where a fictional dad says something profound about catching a ball. This isn't weakness. This is nature. Your brain and heart are syncing up to make room for the kind of emotional bandwidth fatherhood requires. Let it happen. Embrace it. These feelings are preview trailers of what's to come — the deep, surprising love that will sneak up on you at random moments. It's all part of the mental remodeling process. So go ahead, tear up while browsing the baby section. Cry during the theme song to *Bluey*. You're not broken — you're becoming a *good dad*.

Build your pregnancy translation dictionary. Pregnancy comes with a rapidly evolving dialect, and if you want to be a helpful partner instead of a confused bystander, you'll need to become fluent. She's not always going to tell you exactly what she needs. In part because she's figuring it out in real-time for herself and partly because words like *"fine"* and *"later"* now carry entirely different meanings depending on the inflection, time of day, or humidity levels. Eventually, you'll master the incredible skill of anticipating her needs before she has to ask. This isn't just helpful — this is your innate, deep-rooted survival instinct at work. It keeps your relationship strong and your partner supported.

THE THIRD TRIMESTER

Welcome to the final stretch!

The belly is no longer a cute bump. It's a full-blown, attention demanding presence. She is officially uncomfortable, sleep is rare, and her shoes have inexplicably shrunk by 3 sizes.

This is the phase where reality starts knocking louder. You'll find yourself buried in to-do lists, birth plans, and diaper stockpiles. You're on the threshold of a life-altering moment, and it's okay if you don't feel 100% ready. *No one does.*

Here's the truth: you're not going to master fatherhood in advance. But if you've made it this far, then you're already doing exactly what you need to.

The finish line is in sight. So breathe, stay flexible, and keep the car gassed up.

BABY SIZE
WEEK 27

"thermos"

Portable. Durable.
May leak.

Chapter 7

Weeks 27-30

The Great Movie Kick

Early in our marriage, Tambi and I decided to forego the distraction of having a TV in the bedroom. This idea was predicated on the notion that the bedroom should be preserved as a sanctuary of intimacy — a place dedicated to precisely two activities: sleeping and one other thing. As I lay in bed one night, it occurred to me that this decision led to predictable results. Directly ahead of me was an empty wall where a 55-inch flat screen could have lived. To my right lay a very pregnant woman.

We had maintained our bedroom as a TV-less space for nearly 5 years, but now that Tambi was in the midst of the 3rd trimester, we had to make some compromises. This was primarily due to the bed being where she was often most comfortable — a place where we could support her ever-expanding body with an ever-expanding system of strategically placed pillows. While we still did not bring a TV into the bedroom, we did start watching the occasional movie on the tablet, propped up on her belly with the help of one of my flannel shirts rolled up as a makeshift kickstand.

Thus far in the pregnancy, we had experienced quite a few interesting developments, but the most recent one is how my wife's taste in movies had dramatically changed. Tambi, whose cinematic preferences typically gravitate toward romantic comedies, had developed a sudden and inexplicable taste for psychological thrillers. The darker and more suspenseful, the better.

"I think it balances out my hormones," she said one night, pressing play on a movie whose opening scene depicted a terrified person who was gagged and tied up in a dark basement. *"The tension somehow relaxes me."*

Personally, I do not find these types of movies relaxing at all, but being the dutiful husband that I am, I soldiered on.

So there we were — one Friday night, in bed, lights off, the room completely dark except for the pale glow of the tablet screen, perched like a miniature drive-in theatre on her abdomen. The only sounds were our breathing and the increasingly unsettling soundtrack of the film.

The suspense was peaking. A lone character, armed only with a flashlight and a poor sense of judgment, was creeping toward a door that absolutely should not be opened.

The music thinned to a whisper.

My heartbeat accelerated.

The entire room felt tight with tension.

We were both holding our breath.

Then, as the character slowly turned the doorknob, *it happened.*

From the depths of Tambi's womb, our unborn daughter issued a kick with the decisive swiftness of a muay thai fighter. In an instant, the tablet launched forward and landed face-down on the comforter — plunging the room into complete darkness.

The following events occurred over the next 3 seconds...

Tambi, having experienced not only the jump-scare from the movie, but simultaneously one emanating from deep within her own body, released a terrible scream. This primordial scream exploded into our pitch-black bedroom with such force that the neighbor's dog started barking, and a portrait on the wall went askew. My wife, being the capable multitasker that she is, was also quite busy kicking, thrashing, and otherwise doing her level best to subdue or at least greatly confuse her non-existent attacker. Unfortunately, her defensive efforts caused the still-face-down tablet to be pushed to a remote corner of the bed.

In the midst of the chaos, I was blindly groping for the lamp on my nightstand. Just as my fingers found the neck of the lamp, Tambi's flailing claws found various tender parts of my anatomy. One set of claws sank into my ribs, another found my neck, and inexplicably, a third latched onto my right hip. Startled by what could only be interpreted as a wolverine attack, I instinctively recoiled. My body jerked backward, my arm swung outward, and my hand — still clutching the lamp — flung it into the void.

Time slowed. In that suspended moment, I could actually hear the lamp cord stretching to its limit, the plug straining against the outlet, and the final, fateful pop as it disconnected completely. The lamp, now airborne and free from its tether, flew majestically across the room before meeting its tragic end, shattering upon impact with my acoustic guitar, which had been peacefully resting in its stand.

With my wife's claws embedded in my flesh and the discordant twang of the guitar still ringing in the air, I managed to find the tablet, flip it over, and restore the screen's soft glow to the room. Our startled expressions, now illuminated, showed a nameless emotion, but one that could be described as the type worn by people who have just survived a life-threatening event.

For a few long seconds, we stared at each other in silence, stunned, hearts pounding, and then both slowly turned our gaze toward the offending belly.

"Was that... her?" I asked.

"She kicked," Tambi said, still recovering. *"I mean, **really** kicked."*

Maybe it was just a coincidence that our daughter launched her attack at the exact moment the movie hit peak suspense. Or perhaps she felt Tambi's heart rate spike, sensed the adrenaline surge, and decided to respond in kind. Either way, it was, without question, a most memorable movie night.

Window To The Womb

By week 29, the gentle flutters and occasional kicks of early pregnancy have evolved into something more dramatic. What she once described as something that felt like a little goldfish bumping around was now more like the coordinated efforts of a creature testing the tensile limits of its fleshy enclosure.

One evening, as we sat on the couch, I witnessed something I still have trouble explaining to people without sounding unwell. My wife's belly, which had become a sort of live-action display case, suddenly produced a sharp, unmistakable protrusion that was clearly visible externally. It moved, slowly but decisively, from left to right, tracing a path across her belly like a dolphin gliding just beneath the surface of the ocean. Except instead of water, it was skin. And instead of a dolphin, it was our daughter's knee or elbow or forehead.

"That's normal, right?" I asked, in the cautious tone of someone not entirely prepared to hear the answer.

"Normal," Tambi replied. *"But it feels so weird."*

I placed my hand where the movement had just been, and to my amazement, little Molly pushed back. An unmistakable nudge against my palm, as if to say, *"Hello, father, just doing some redecorating in here."* We stayed like that for a moment, hand to belly, communicating through this bizarre epidermal interface like two travelers from vastly different realms trying to reach an understanding through the universal language of touch.

This stage of pregnancy is where your baby begins to hint at having a personality. Ours, we learned, had preferences. She moved more in the evenings. She disliked lying down. She would respond to certain music and voices. My voice, in particular, which I found flattering.

It was strange and beautiful and, at times, vaguely unsettling. A tiny human was in there, fully alive, shifting position, stretching limbs, testing boundaries, both literally and figuratively. It was the first time I realized we weren't just expecting a baby. We were already living with one.

Pregnancy Bladder

Through close observation and consultation with my pregnant wife, I've constructed a vividly realistic scenario to help you, dear reader, empathize with the unique, maddening, and increasingly urgent bladder challenges faced by pregnant women.

I call it *"A Mental Experiment in Urinary Futility."*

Let's begin, shall we?

Think back to that time you drank a gallon of water because you were *"hydrating for health,"* or maybe knocked back a few too many beers with the fellas. Either way, you know the feeling I'm talking about. That deep, pulsing urgency that signals to your brain that your bladder is rapidly approaching its maximum volumetric capacity. It's not a subtle feeling. It's the kind of pressure that commandeers your entire body, overrides all other thoughts, and turns taking a leak into a non-negotiable mission of utmost importance.

In response to this feeling, your mind shifts instantly into a kind of primal crisis mode. You rapidly analyze all available locations for answering the call of nature within reasonable proximity. Bathroom? *Too far.* Port-a-potty? *Questionable, but acceptable if desperate.* Tree line? *Promising, if you keep your back to the wind.* You calculate distance, foot traffic, concealment, lighting conditions, and the likelihood of unexpected witnesses, all within seconds. Once a location is decided upon, you relocate and make your move — unzipping with the confidence of a man seconds away from one of life's simplest and most satisfying pleasures.

Ready.

Aim.

Fire?

Nothing happens.

Well, not nothing exactly, but not at all what you were expecting. Instead of the mighty, unrelenting stream you've come to rely on throughout a lifetime of successful urination, you release... half a thimble-full. Barely enough to dampen its dainty interior.

And yet, even though you've seemingly drained you're bulging bladder, the feeling of fullness remains. The pressure is still there. The urgency, undiminished.

So, you try again. A single, defiant, golden droplet emerges, and then... *nothing.* Your body has betrayed you. Your bladder swore it was full, but it's become a liar. A trickster. A false prophet.

Now, repeat this scenario every half-hour. All day. And again, a dozen or so times per night. That's life with pregnancy bladder.

Interestingly, her bladder hasn't technically gotten any smaller. But the ever-growing uterus — the bladder's cantankerous next-door neighbor — is expanding in every direction, pressing more and more on all surrounding organs, including the humble bladder.

So yes, she's going to the bathroom a lot. And yes, oftentimes, it's for what amounts to a ceremonial drizzle. Don't question it. Don't suggest she *"try going less often."* Definitely don't joke about it unless you want to be introduced to a different kind of biological urgency — the kind in which you're tasked with deftly maneuvering your cranium from the path of high-speed flying objects.

Baby Status Update

At this stage, your baby is roughly the size of a classic thermos — you know, the heavy-duty green kind that looks like it was carved from a billet of aluminum and could survive a fall from low orbit. Strangely fitting, really. Both are rugged, dependable, and destined to be with you for the long haul. One warms soup, the other warms your soul.

Movements are more pronounced now. You'll be able to see and feel kicks, rolls, and stretches from the outside. These movements may start to follow a more predictable pattern, often increasing in the evenings. Some kicks may even cause visible shifts or lumps under the skin, which can be fascinating or even slightly unsettling.

Internally, the baby's lungs, brain, and nervous system are rapidly developing. The lungs are starting to produce surfactant, a substance that helps them stay open after birth, making it easier for them to take their first breath of fresh air. Their senses are becoming more active, especially hearing. They can now recognize familiar voices and sounds, which means it's a good time to start talking to the baby regularly — a practice that will make you feel utterly ridiculous at first but quickly becomes second nature. I started off feeling like I was auditioning for a role in a particularly cheesy commercial, awkwardly leaning toward my wife's belly button and saying things like, "*Hello in there... it's... uh... Dad.*" My wife found this endlessly entertaining.

This stage is also when you start to get a clearer sense of your baby's temperament. How active they are, what seems to stimulate them, and when they're most alert. These little clues, while not definitive, are the beginning of getting to know the little person you'll soon meet.

Action Steps

Schedule a hospital tour and pre-register. The last thing you want during active labor is to be filling out insurance forms while your partner threatens bodily harm for every contraction that passes. Book your hospital tour now. These fill up quickly, and you want time to process what you learn. During the tour, take notes on practical logistics: parking options *(including after-hours)*, which entrance to use when you arrive, ID requirements, and visitor policies. Note where the ice machines, snack options, and coffee are located — seemingly trivial details that become somewhat more important during a 20-hour labor. After the tour, complete all pre-registration paperwork. Create a folder with copies of your insurance cards, birth plan, and any hospital forms. The goal is to reduce the administrative burden when you arrive on the big day to *"here's our paperwork"* rather than *"what's our policy number again?"*

Plan "Fourth Trimester" Meals. The fourth trimester *(those first 12 weeks after birth)* is a survival period where cooking proper meals becomes a distant memory. Start stocking your freezer now with easy, nutritious options. The key is variety. Don't make eight lasagnas unless you want to hate lasagna with burning passion by week three. Focus on meals that can be eaten one-handed *(new parent skill #1)*, provide good nutrition for healing and milk production, and don't require complicated reheating. If cooking isn't your thing, research meal delivery services or create a meal train sign-up sheet for friends and family to use after the baby arrives.

Enjoy being just the two of you. The countdown to the baby's arrival has started in earnest, making this the perfect time to prioritize experiences that will become logistically challenging with a newborn. Make a list of restaurants, movies, weekend trips, or activities you've been meaning to enjoy. Schedule a proper date night at least once every two weeks. Not just dinner, but events that create memories: concerts, theater shows, or that cooking class you've talked about trying. Take *"before baby"* photos that aren't focused on her belly — just the two of you enjoying each other's company. These aren't frivolous indulgences; they're investments in your relationship before it undergoes its most significant transition. The strongest foundation for your growing family is a solid partnership between the two of you, and intentional connection now pays dividends during the challenging newborn period.

Research birth photography options. Whether you hire a professional or handle documentation yourself, now is the time to create a plan. If considering a professional birth photographer, interview candidates who specialize in birth specifically. It requires different skills from wedding or portrait photography. Ask about their backup plans, on-call policies, and experience working in your chosen birth setting. If planning to photograph the birth yourself, invest in proper equipment: a camera with good low-light capabilities, extra batteries, and sufficient memory cards. Research hospital policies about photography during different stages of labor and delivery. Create a shot list of moments you don't want to miss. Even if formal photography isn't your style, establish a plan for capturing those first precious moments.

BABY SIZE
WEEK 31
"football"

Go long!
Just kidding.

Chapter 8
Weeks 31-35
Human Nesting Instinct

Nesting, in the wild, is elegant, purposeful, and instinctual. A seamless part of nature's blueprint for survival.

Take the satin bowerbird, for example. The male carefully constructs a tunnel-like structure made of twigs, which he then obsessively decorates with all manner of blue-colored objects. Berries, flowers, bottle caps, string — anything he can find to make the nest more blue. Meanwhile, sea turtles will travel thousands of miles across literal oceans to return to the very beach where they were born. Driven purely by innate instinct, they'll crawl well above the high tide waterline, dig a hole, and lay their eggs before vanishing back into the sea. The Arctic fox will excavate an elaborate multi-room den with separate, purpose-built chambers for raising pups, storing food, and surviving in the middle of a frozen wasteland.

Then there's us.

Human nesting lacks natural elegance. We do not simply feel the pull of nature and act. Instead, we operate based on a complex system of line items, sticky notes, and color-coded tabs.

My role was clearly defined: I was the muscle. My task was to methodically work my way through a detailed to-do list that Tambi had meticulously crafted. On that list were categories such as *"Must Do Before Birth"*, *"Would Be Nice"*, and a particularly ominous section labeled, *"Don't Make Me Ask Again."*

I approached the list with the grim resolve of a man who understood that failure was not an option. My motivation wasn't just moral — it was medical — based on direct orders from the doctor concerning my wife's activity level: *"No heavy lifting. Minimal exertion. Take it easy."* She delivered these words while staring directly into my eyes, and did not break that gaze until I confirmed receipt of the message with a solemn nod.

I was prepared to make every effort to get our home baby-ready while following the Doc's explicit orders, but what I hadn't anticipated was the raw, gravitational force of Tambi's nesting instinct. Despite medical guidance and despite her best intentions, she often could not stop herself. One afternoon, I came home to find her on the counter, sleeves rolled up, aggressively dusting the top of the refrigerator.

"Honey," I said, slowly approaching as if she were a spooked jumper on a hotel balcony, *"what are you doing?"*

"I'm taking it easy," she replied, as if the words themselves could disguise the fact that I was in the presence of a barefoot pregnant woman standing on the kitchen countertop.

This was clearly not a woman who could be reasoned with. This was a force of nature. A woman hellbent on winning a war of attrition against the ever-growing to-do list.

Thus was my motivation. I knew that if I slowed down, if I faltered, if I procrastinated, she would be quick to fill in the gaps. Her pace was motivational in the same way that a landslide is motivational — get moving or get buried.

I got moving.

Each finished project wasn't just another checkmark on the list — it was a kind of protective barrier against Tambi attempting something she shouldn't. And I began to take a strange, quiet pride in it. Installing curtain rods? *Check*. Painting the closet shelves? *Check*. Shampooing the carpets? *Check*.

"You know," she said one evening, as I collapsed beside her on the bed after fully assembling the crib with only seven bolts left over, *"I really appreciate how hard you're working. I just wish I could help more."*

"Your job is growing our daughter," I reminded her, pressing my hand gently to her belly. Tambi smiled, and right on cue, a little foot pressed back through her skin like a high five.

O Comfort, Where Art Thou?

At this stage, physical comfort becomes increasingly elusive. Your partner may be dealing with a rotating cast of symptoms. Back pain, round ligament pain, swelling in the hands and feet, persistent heartburn, shortness of breath, and general fatigue, all layered atop one another. Even simple movements like standing up from a chair, rolling over in bed, or putting on shoes can feel like a monumental challenge.

What's even trickier is that it can all vary from day to day. Some mornings, she might feel okay, but by the afternoon, her joints ache, and her feet are twice their normal size. On top of that, the extra weight she's carrying can throw off her center of gravity, which makes even casual household tasks far more difficult than they appear.

How to support her:

Handle the physical errands. Carry groceries, vacuum, and bend down to pick things up for her. Be patient when she moves slowly, cancels plans, or gets overwhelmed by seemingly small things.

Help her find more comfortable sitting or sleeping positions, even if it means becoming an expert in pillow geometry. Offer back rubs, foot rubs, or warm compresses. Whatever she finds is most soothing for her aches and pains.

Pregnancy is physically demanding in a way that's impossible to comprehend unless you're the one experiencing it. Even on days when she insists she's *"fine,"* her body is doing a job that requires constant effort. Small gestures, especially the quiet, thoughtful ones, can go a long way toward making her feel seen, comforted, and supported.

Sleep Challenges

Sleep, already complicated by the second trimester, enters new territory now. It's not just about quantity anymore. It's about managing the quality of whatever fragments she can get here and there. Between frequent bathroom trips, an increasingly limited number of viable sleeping positions, baby gymnastics at midnight, and general discomfort, full nights of uninterrupted sleep can become a rare luxury.

You might notice new habits start to form. She may begin dozing off earlier in the evening, napping in awkward positions during the day, or switching between the bed, couch, and glider in search of relief. A once semi-predictable bedtime routine now involves an ever-evolving combination of pillows, stretches, experimental positions, and heating/cooling pads.

Your role isn't to fix her sleep. You can't. But you can help create a sleep-friendly environment.

Keep the bedroom comfortable, dark, and quiet. Invest in blackout curtains or a white noise machine if needed. Have spare pillows and soft blankets nearby so she can experiment with different positions and support systems. Be mindful of your sleep habits — snoring, tossing, turning, or even just crowding her space can push her over the edge. Encourage her to rest whenever the opportunity presents itself, regardless of what time of day it is.

Sleep deprivation will affect you both, and that's kind of part of the package. Consider it training for the main event. The goal right now is flexibility. Building a household rhythm that honors rest when and where it happens. Even short naps or moments of stillness can make a big difference.

Self-Care for Dads-To-Be

You might feel like you're in constant "*go mode*" right now. Holding down a job, running errands, building baby furniture, managing finances, and loads more. There's a creeping pressure to get everything done before the baby arrives, and while it's good to stay productive, it's easy to forget that you're also going through a major transition. You're not just helping someone else become a parent. You're becoming one yourself.

This can bring on a strange mix of emotions. Excitement, yes. But also anxiety, fear, and doubt. You may find yourself wondering if you're actually ready for all this responsibility or whether you're cut out to be a dad. Those thoughts are not a sign of failure. They're a sign that you're taking it seriously.

It's essential, especially in this final stretch, to make space for your own emotional health. That doesn't mean disappearing for hours or avoiding your responsibilities. It means being intentional about checking in with yourself and permitting yourself to feel what you're feeling.

Start with the basics:

Move your body. You don't have to train for a marathon or break personal records at the gym. But getting your body in motion, even just a brisk 15-minute walk around the block, can work wonders. Physical movement helps release built-up stress, clears mental fog, and reminds your nervous system that you're not stuck. Stretch in the mornings. Breathe deeply. All of these things help your mind and body reset.

Talk to someone. This doesn't have to be a deep, soul-baring monologue. It can be as simple as a text to a friend that says, *"Hey, this is harder than I thought."* Or telling your partner, *"I'm feeling a bit off today."* Fatherhood can be isolating if you let it be. Naming your stress out loud, even in the simplest terms, can immediately lessen its grip.

Step away from the lists. The to-do list will still be there tomorrow. Give yourself an evening where you don't check off a single task. Close the baby registry tab. Don't Google *"best bottle sterilizer."* Watch a dumb movie. Play a video game. Order takeout.

Do something that reminds you you're still you, not just a checklist-attacking machine.

Get rest when you can. Fatigue has a way of distorting everything. Small problems feel massive, minor irritations spark arguments, and your ability to be present, kind, and helpful takes a nosedive. Rest is not laziness. It's not indulgent. It's not something you *"earn"* after crossing everything off the to-do list. It's maintenance. Preventative care. Mental armor. You'll be far better for everyone if you're rested, clear-headed, and well-functioning.

Give your brain a breather. Not everything in your life has to revolve around the baby. Read something completely unrelated. Journal a few thoughts in the morning. Sit outside with your phone on airplane mode. Listen to music that has nothing to do with lullabies. You're allowed to remain a whole person during this time. In fact, your child needs you to.

And perhaps most importantly, **be honest with your partner**.

You don't need to pretend to be unshakable. In fact, trying to appear invincible might create more distance at a time when you both need connection the most. Let her know when you're struggling. Let her reassure you. Let her laugh with you by admitting that your series of baby-related YouTube searches led you to a video on *"how to swaddle a burrito."*

Becoming a *good dad* doesn't happen all at once. It's not a light switch. It's a slow, messy, wonderful evolution — and you're already deep into it! Take care of yourself so you can show up fully for the people who will need you most in the weeks ahead.

Baby Status Update

We've officially entered the stage where most pregnancy books would begin comparing your baby to various types of large melons. I, however, will refrain because certain features of your partner's anatomy may already resemble a pair of particularly well-hydrated cantaloupes, and I have too much class to go down that road. Instead, I'll compare your pure, innocent child to a football. Yes, a brown, pointy-ended, inflated hunk of swine epidermis. Approximately 15 inches long and around 3 pounds, your baby has now officially reached *"Super Bowl snack table centerpiece"* proportions.

This is one of the most critical phases for neurological development. Brain growth is accelerating. The lungs are maturing. If born now, the baby would likely need medical support, but their chances of survival are very high. They can hear, recognize familiar voices, and respond to sound and light. Movement is strong and frequent. Punches, kicks, rolls, and stretches are normal, even if they look a bit alarming from the outside. The baby's running out of room, but they're not done growing yet!

Action Steps

With the finish line on the horizon, weeks 31-35 bring a new sense of urgency. Here's what needs your focused attention now.

Install your car seat. This seemingly simple task requires more preparation than you might think. Start by researching which type meets your needs: infant-only seat versus convertible, budget versus premium features. Once purchased, schedule an appointment with a certified Car Seat Safety Technician *(many fire stations, hospitals, or police departments offer this service for* *free)*. For most red-blooded males, this step may seem superfluous, but studies show that over 80% of car seats are installed incorrectly by well-meaning parents. Even if you think you've got it right, professional verification ensures your precious cargo travels safely.

Pack those hospital bags. Don't wait until contractions are five minutes apart to throw random items into a duffel bag. Create separate, clearly labeled bags: one for labor, one for the postpartum stay, and one specifically for you. The labor bag should contain comfort items *(massage tools, music speaker, her pillow)*, toiletries, labor aids *(birthing ball, cooling spray, lip balm)*, and a comfortable outfit for her to labor in. The postpartum bag needs nursing supplies, comfortable loose clothing, phone chargers, and outfits for the baby's trip home. Your bag deserves equal attention: change of clothes, toiletries, snacks, entertainment for long labor hours, caffeinated beverages, and a pillow if you're planning to sleep in the hospital room. Pack a separate small wallet with only essentials *(ID, insurance card, some cash)* rather than your entire everyday wallet that contains your library card, hardware store loyalty punch card, and receipts from 2019.

Complete essential nursery setup. While Pinterest-perfect nurseries can wait, certain elements need to be functional before the baby arrives. Assemble the crib or bassinet according to current safety guidelines *(no bumpers, pillows, or stuffed animals)*, ensuring it meets all safety standards. Install blackout curtains. They're not just aesthetic, they're invaluable for encouraging daytime naps. Set up a proper changing station with supplies organized in easy reach of the changing surface. You'll be doing this sleep-deprived and potentially one-handed, so efficiency matters. Create a comfortable feeding station with supportive seating, a side table for supplies, and good lighting. Add a white noise machine and night light with dim settings.

Practice essential labor support techniques. Being an effective birth partner requires more than just showing up and holding her hand. Research and practice specific comfort measures. Counter-pressure for back labor, hip squeezes for pelvic pain, effective massage techniques for different labor stages, and proper assistance for various laboring positions. Learn breathing patterns so you can guide her through them during intense contractions. Practice using a birth ball or peanut ball to support different positions. If you've taken childbirth classes, review your notes and materials now. Create a small reference card with key reminders about what helps during different labor stages. Your confident support during labor isn't just nice to have — it can significantly impact her birth experience and your shared memory of this momentous day.

Develop your postpartum support plan. The initial weeks after birth require more support than most new parents anticipate. Create a detailed plan that goes beyond vague offers of help. Establish a visitor policy that protects your family bonding time while allowing meaningful support. Create a chore chart dividing essential household tasks between you and any helping family members. Set up meal delivery schedules using an app like *"Meal Train,"* where friends can sign up for specific dates. Prepare a list of specific tasks people can help with when they ask, *"What can I do?"* Think along the lines of: laundry, dog walking, grocery shopping, house cleaning, dish washing, etc. The more concrete your plan, the less you'll need to coordinate while sleep-deprived, and the more likely you'll actually receive the help you need rather than a house full of visitors expecting to be entertained while admiring your baby.

BABY SIZE WEEK 36
"babydoll"

The likeness is uncanny.

Chapter 9

Weeks 36-40

False Alarm

At the beginning of pregnancy, you tend to think in terms of trimesters. It's the largest block of time by which the progression of pregnancy can be measured. As time progresses, though, you'll gradually shift to thinking in incrementally smaller units of time. Months, weeks, days, hours, and eventually, even minutes.

For me, one of these time-altering shifts occurred around week 37. It was early morning or late night, depending on your definition of 2:15 AM. Tambi was having trouble sleeping. We were in the kitchen. A kettle of water was heating up for tea. I was scooping a spoonful of peanut butter from the jar when Tambi casually said, *"You know, if the baby came now, she'd likely be just fine."*

I paused. Spoon hovering between the jar and my open mouth. The realization that the baby could potentially arrive at any moment rolled over me with the force of a slow-motion freight train. Up until now, I'd been mentally floating in a haze of *"sometime in the relatively near future."* But suddenly, I had to confront the reality that this was no longer an eventuality — it was an inevitability. A

107

soon-to-happen event with no semblance of a clearly defined schedule.

I wish I could say that I responded to Tambi's remark with calm resolve. Perhaps a confident, *"We're ready when the baby is,"* just as the peanut butter spoon landed upon my tongue. Instead, I stood motionless, peanut butter spoon slowly falling further and further from my mouth, while my brain short-circuited like a toaster dropped in the bathtub. As the enormity of it all sank in, the kettle began to whistle.

Later that day, I transformed into a man gripped by purpose — albeit the vague, slightly manic kind. I roamed the house with the urgency of someone preparing for a surprise inspection by the Department of Parenthood. I checked expiration dates on pantry items like we were hosting a food safety seminar. I tested the baby monitor despite the apparent absence of a baby to monitor. I finally took the car seat out of the trunk, where it had lived, unopened, for more than three months, and installed it. Then I uninstalled it, rotated it 180 degrees, and installed it correctly.

It wasn't panic, exactly. It was more like a sudden and overwhelming realization that we were gradually toeing up to an invisible line that, at some unknown point in the near future, we would cross.

The Weight Of Fatherhood

There's a point in late pregnancy when the mental load catches up with you. It's no longer just about stocking up on diapers or assembling the bassinet. It's about the sheer magnitude of what's coming. The car seat is installed. Your bags are packed. You've had the hospital tour, memorized the alternate routes, and loaded your favorite snacks into the glove box. And still, there's this lingering sense of *"Are we ready for this?"*

This is when many dads-to-be start feeling the full psychological weight of impending fatherhood. It's the transition from *"expectant"* to *"responsible."* You might catch yourself zoning out while brushing your teeth, imagining scenarios where you're suddenly left alone with the baby and expected to know what to do. You stare into the crib and think, *"A baby will be lying in there soon. One that belongs to me."*

The good news is you don't have to be perfect. You don't even have to feel ready because it's not about having all the answers. It's about being present in the uncertainty. Being the steady hand when your partner needs help. Being the fresh set of eyes when exhaustion blurs hers. Being the person who says, *"We'll figure this out,"* and genuinely means it, even when you're not sure how.

You'll forget things. You'll make mistakes. You'll have moments where you feel entirely out of your depth. But you'll also adapt. You'll get better. You'll grow into this role the way every *good dad* before you has: by doing it, one imperfect day at a time. If you can offer that — your focus, your energy, your heart — the rest tends to fall into place.

Braxton Hicks

With a gentle shake of my shoulder, I opened my eyes to find Tambi sitting up in bed next to me. Her voice was low and steady when she spoke.

"I'm having contractions."

I sat bolt upright as if a small detonation had occurred beneath the mattress. My heart rate spiked, my pupils dilated, and I turned toward the digital clock glowing dimly on the nightstand. 3:17 A.M. I specifically recall feeling resentment toward the clock, as if it had known all along that this was the moment labor would begin, but had smugly chosen to withhold this information.

The following turn of events could best be described as a masterclass in well-meaning incompetence.

I lunged for the contraction timer app on my phone — an app I had downloaded eight-and-a-half months ago and was now opening for the first time. I had no idea how it worked, but I mashed buttons like I was trying to crack a high-security cipher. This effort was quickly abandoned for more familiar territory. I redirected my efforts to frantically searching for the car keys, which I eventually found in the least likely location imaginable: the wall hook where we keep the car keys. Unfortunately, during the subsequent blur of checking the hospital bag, inspecting the car seat installation, and mentally preparing for a high-speed getaway, the keys managed to disappear and reappear no fewer than three times. Every few minutes, I diligently returned to Tambi to ask, *"Are you okay?"* which, to her credit, she answered with increasing patience — until the seventeenth time, when her eyes narrowed in a way that suggested that I might soon be the one to experience physical discomfort.

And then, just as abruptly as they'd begun, the contractions stopped.

Poof. Gone.

We sat there for a while, waiting to see if they'd return. They didn't.

It was a classic false alarm. Braxton Hicks, they call them. The irritatingly convincing *"practice"* contractions that exist solely to test your reflexes and threaten your sanity. Tambi, tired but composed, crawled back into bed and quickly went back to sleep. I, on the other hand, lay flat on my back, staring wide-eyed at the ceiling in the dark. My nervous system still ringing like a fire bell. My shirt was inside out. My mouth, inexplicably dry. I felt like I'd aged several years in a matter of minutes.

It wouldn't be the last time we mistook Braxton Hicks for the real thing, but it was a helpful dress rehearsal. The kind that makes you realize this isn't a hypothetical scenario anymore. It's happening. Not now, but soon.

False Alarms, Real Stress

One of the biggest psychological hurdles during these final weeks is navigating the ever-frustrating, constantly misleading, and occasionally terrifying landscape of false alarms. Every time she feels something new — an odd cramp, a tightening across her belly, a weird internal shift — you'll both find yourselves suddenly asking, *"Is this it?"*

All times except one, of course, it's not. Just another Braxton Hicks contraction. A trial run by the uterus, like a fire drill conducted in the middle of the night with no warning and no fire. These *"practice contractions"* are your partner's body rehearsing for the main event. They tend to be irregular, not too painful, and may fade if she changes position or drinks water.

But knowing the technical difference between Braxton Hicks and real labor doesn't make the experience any less stressful. It's hard to sleep soundly when your partner jolts upright in the middle of the

111

night with a strange look on her face and starts a timer on her phone.

Your job is to stay calm and prepared. This means keeping your phone charged and nearby, topping off the gas tank regularly, and not venturing too far from home without a backup plan. And above all, listen. If she says something feels different, trust that. Even if it turns out to be a false alarm, your responsiveness will matter. These moments are tests. Not of your medical knowledge, but of your readiness and your ability to remain steadfast when things feel uncertain.

What to Watch For

At your partner's prenatal appointments, the doctor may begin checking for cervical dilation *(how open the cervix is)* and effacement *(how thin it's become)*. These are indicators that her body is prepping for labor, but annoyingly, they do not tell you *when* it will happen. A woman can be 3 centimeters dilated for weeks, or go from zero to delivery in a matter of hours. Labor does not follow a script.

Here are the signs to watch for:

Regular, intensifying contractions: True labor contractions follow a pattern, grow closer together, and become more painful. They do not go away with a change in position or a glass of water.

Water breaking: This could be a dramatic Hollywood-style gush or a slow, confusing trickle. Either way, it's a tell-tale sign to call the doctor and prepare to head in.

Consistent lower back pain: Especially if it doesn't change with movement or position. Back labor is real, and it's often a fairly reliable early indicator.

The "bloody show": Despite the ominous name, this simply refers to the loss of the mucus plug, often tinged with blood. It's a sign that the cervix is dilating — but again, it could still be days *(or longer)* before labor begins.

The takeaway? Stay informed, stay calm, and remember that no question is too small or silly to ask your care provider. This is not the time for pride or guesswork. This is the time for clear communication and readiness.

Baby Status Update

By now, the whole *"your baby is the size of a [insert random object]"* gimmick has officially run its course. Earlier comparisons to hacky sacks and donuts felt charming and whimsical, but now we're deep into the third trimester. Things are getting serious. While your partner's belly might suggest she's smuggling a beach ball, a countertop bread maker, or a gently used Toyota Prius — chances are that your baby is now roughly the size of, well... *a baby*. A soon-to-be-diaper-demolishing human being. Approximately 6 to 9 pounds, 18 to 21 inches long, and fully capable of causing spontaneous weeping just by curling their tiny fingers around yours.

By weeks 36 through 40, your baby is officially full-term and ready *(or almost ready)* to make their grand entrance. Most babies settle into the head-down position by this point — a fact your provider will monitor closely. If your baby is still breech *(feet or bottom down)*, your care team may discuss techniques to help them turn or make a plan for delivery.

Movements may feel less like sharp kicks and more like long, slow stretches. Physically, your baby is putting on fat, strengthening breathing muscles, and fine-tuning essential skills like sucking and swallowing. Brain development continues rapidly even in these final days, which is one of the reasons many doctors prefer not to induce unless medically necessary. These final days in the womb are invaluable for overall development, so it's not something to rush unless there's a good reason to do so.

Emotionally, this stage can feel like the quiet before the storm. You're on the edge of everything, staring down the barrel of a seismic life shift. You might not feel ready, but trust this:

Readiness isn't just a checklist. It's a mental state. It's staying present, paying attention, maintaining a sense of calm, and being willing to adapt to whatever comes next. Your baby will arrive when the time is right. And when they do, they'll be meeting a *good dad* who's vastly more prepared and capable than he realizes.

Action Steps

You've reached the home stretch! With the countdown to launch ticking more and more loudly, here's what needs your attention during weeks 36-40.

Set up a complete sleeping station for your newborn. The official recommendation is that babies sleep in their parents' room *(but not in their bed)* for at least the first six months. Position the bassinet or crib within arm's reach of your bed but away from windows, cords, and heating vents. Install a dim night light that provides just enough illumination for nighttime feedings and diaper changes without fully waking the baby. Prepare multiple bassinet sheets and waterproof mattress covers for inevitable middle-of-the-night accidents. Stock a nearby drawer with diapers, wipes, changes of clothes, and feeding supplies so you don't have to wander the house at 3 AM. More than just convenience, a proper sleep setup directly impacts safety, rest, and establishing healthy sleep patterns from the beginning.

Create work handoff documentation. Whether you're taking two weeks or two months of leave, proper preparation prevents your paternity leave from being interrupted by work emergencies. Identify and train a specific person to handle different aspects of your role. Set up email auto-responses with clear information about your absence duration, return date, and who to contact for what issues. Schedule a proper handoff meeting before your departure rather than hastily explaining things on your last day. Establish boundaries around when *(if at all)* you'll check messages or take calls during leave. Being thorough now means you can be fully present during this irreplaceable time with your new family without workplace stress undermining these precious weeks.

Establish visitor guidelines. The postpartum period requires careful boundary-setting before emotions and exhaustion cloud your judgment. Create specific visitor policies: when you'll accept visitors, how long they can stay, and what you expect from them *(hint: it's bringing food and doing chores, not expecting to be entertained)*. Designate a point person *(not you or your partner)* who can update friends and family, fielding the inevitable flood of *"any news yet?"* messages. Prepare a standard response for unwanted visit requests. Consider something like: *"We're taking these first few days to bond as a family and establish breastfeeding. We'll let you know when we're ready for visitors."* It's about protecting your family's adjustment period and your partner's physical recovery during an intensely vulnerable time.

Chapter 10
The Birth

Tuesday. 5:52 A.M.

I was awakened by the sound of Tambi easing herself out of bed. This, in and of itself, was not at all unusual. Bathroom trips occurring several times an hour had been her new normal for the last few months. What did catch my attention, however, was how she lingered next to the bed. In the dim, early morning light, I could just make out her silhouette — standing still, arms low, gently patting at her upper thighs with a kind of puzzled hesitation. Something about it told me this wasn't just another twilight waddle to the toilet.

"I think... my water broke?"

She said these words with a tone of uncertainty.

I launched from bed, sprinted to the bathroom, grabbed a towel, folded it into a thick pad, and applied it to my leaky bride. In the 1.8 seconds it took me to accomplish this maneuver, what had begun as a minor trickle had quickly escalated into a voluminous deluge, which confirmed her initial suspicion.

"OH MY — YEAH, IT BROKE, IT BROKE!" she said.

This was in no way news to me, as my reply was...

"I KNOW, I KNOW — IT'S RUNNING DOWN MY ARM!"

We both waddled to the bathroom in synchronized unison. She led the way while I followed closely behind her, holding the rapidly saturating towel to her backside as she maintained its position on her frontside.

"WHAT DO WE DO NOW!?!?" I inquired.

"We have time," she said calmly. *"Early labor can take hours. Let's wait until the contractions are closer together."*

How could she be so stoic? *THE BABY WAS COMING!*

"Maybe you should take a shower," she suggested, taking notice of my shaking hands, dripping with warm amniotic fluid. *"And eat something. It's going to be a long day."*

What I realized in that pivotal moment was that my wife had just undergone a profound psychological shift. The Tambi I knew — the version I'd come to recognize by her groans, her swollen feet, her body aches, and her insatiable food cravings, was gone. In her place stood an altered version. Sharpened. Focused. Resolute. The launch sequence had been activated, and with it, a deep-rooted, instinctual program seemed to boot up inside her. She moved with a calm resolve that starkly contrasted the chaos I felt rising in my chest. There was a fiery peace in her eyes that told me she wasn't just unafraid of the unstoppable biological process that was underway — *she was ready for it.* I didn't know it at the time, but this was just the prologue to what would soon become one of the most powerful and humbling experiences of my life

The Stages of Labor

You've probably heard that labor comes in *"stages."* In reality, labor is more like a train that slowly gains speed and doesn't stop accelerating until there's a baby in your arms. Still, the idea of stages has stood the test of time. From early humans hunkered in caves to modern hospital rooms, the process remains surprisingly consistent. Here's a breakdown of what you're likely to experience.

STAGE ONE: Early Labor → Active Labor

This is the longest and most varied phase. The cervix begins to dilate *(open)* and efface *(thin out)*, which allows the baby to start moving down into position. At first, contractions may feel like mild cramps or lower back aches. Uncomfortable, but manageable. These can be irregular and spaced out at first *(10–20 minutes apart)*, and they might go on for hours, sometimes an entire day or more. This is why there's no particular rush early on.

Eventually, things shift into *active labor*, where contractions become more intense, longer in duration *(about 45–60 seconds)*, and closer together *(about 3–5 minutes apart)*. This is the point where breathing techniques, focus, and comfort measures *(showers, massage, counterpressure, rocking, etc.)* really come into play. Externally, you can tell she's having a contraction when she goes quiet, focuses inward, or becomes irritable — all of which are good signs that mean her body is doing its job.

What You Do:

Your number one job through the process is to stay calm. Not fake-calm. Not anxious-calm. *Actual* calm. If you radiate panic in any way, she will pick up on it, and that's the last thing she needs on her mind.

Time the contractions with an app. Make sure she's drinking water and nibbling on something (unless told otherwise by a provider). Offer a heating pad. Rub her back. Apply counterpressure on her hips if she asks. Or don't. She'll let you know. Expect her to change her mind. Comfort measures that were miraculous five minutes ago may suddenly become intolerable. Go with it. You are not here to fix anything. You are here to support.

This stage doesn't have a neat timeline, so keep checking in with your provider. The general rule of thumb is the *"5-1-1 Rule"*: contractions that are **five** minutes apart, **one** minute long, and have been that way for **one** hour. That's usually your cue to head for the hospital or birth center. But again, your provider will give the final word. Some first-time moms labor at home for a long time. Others progress faster than expected.

STAGE TWO: Pushing and Delivery

By now, you should be happily settled in at the hospital or birth center. If not — well, I hope you have plenty of towels and that you're good under pressure.

Once the cervix is fully dilated *(10 centimeters)*, it's time to push. This is the part most people imagine when they think of labor. This stage typically lasts anywhere from 2 to 8 hours, and it gets more intense as time goes on.

She'll push with each contraction, often with encouragement from the doctor, nurse, or midwife. Pushing is physical, emotional, and utterly consuming. It's also strangely rhythmic, following the rise and fall of each contraction. She'll push with everything she's got, then rest in between. Then do it again. And again. And again. You'll see her draw on strength you've never witnessed before. It's primal, raw, astonishing, and will forever change the way you see her.

As the baby descends, you'll hear terms like *"crowning,"* and you might see more of the delivery than you ever imagined, anticipated, or intended. If you're squeamish, my suggestion would be to stay north of the equator.

What You Do:

Stay close and be present. That means offering your full attention, tuning into her cues, and staying engaged even during the quieter, repetitive moments when nothing particularly cinematic is happening. Stand beside her. Hold her hand. Wipe her brow. Tell her she's doing an incredible job, even if she's mid-contraction and the only response you get is a pained look that could melt paint. That's okay, because this isn't about your validation. It's about using your calm and reassuring presence to say: *I'm here. I'm in this with you, and I'm not going anywhere.*

The Birth

Eventually, you'll see the baby's head emerge, followed by the shoulders. Then, with one more mighty push, your baby emerges — squirming, slick, and loudly expressing their opinion about the state of things. You may notice that time does a weird thing at this moment. It slows down and speeds up all at once. You'll hear the cry. See your partner collapse in exhausted triumph. Watch the medical team move with practiced precision while your brain tries to reboot and assign meaning to the indescribable spectacle that just unfolded.

STAGE THREE: Delivering the Placenta

The baby is out, but labor isn't quite over. The uterus still needs to expel the placenta, which typically happens within 5 to 30 minutes after delivery. Your partner may have a few more contractions to help this process along, though they're usually much milder.

The doctor or midwife will check to make sure the placenta is delivered intact and that bleeding is under control. You may not notice much of this happening as your attention will likely be locked on your new baby or on trying to remember how to speak in complete sentences again.

What You Do:

Stay present and supportive. She's just done something incredible.

Help hold the baby if she needs rest or medical attention. Take in the moment. You're officially a parent!

One More Thing: There's No "Right Way" It Unfolds

Sometimes, labor skips around a little. Some partners go from barely dilated to pushing in a matter of hours. Others have long, drawn-out early labor with speedy delivery. And sometimes, unexpected interventions or detours (like inductions or C-sections) happen. That's all okay.

Your job isn't to control the process. It's to stay grounded while everything else is in motion. Breathe. Support. Listen. Be there.

Because that, more than anything, is what your partner and your baby will need from you most.

Hands-On?

If you're feeling brave, curious, or simply compelled to have a front-row seat at your transformation into a parent, talk to your provider *before* the big moment. Let them know you'd like to be more hands-on during the delivery, and ask what's possible in your specific setting.

Birth teams are generally supportive of this, provided everything is going smoothly and safely. In many hospitals and birth centers, it's not unusual for the non-birthing partner to take a more active role.

This can include things like:

Cutting the umbilical cord: Once the baby is out and breathing, someone needs to sever the connection to the placenta. That someone could be you, if you're up for it. You'll be handed a pair of sterile scissors and directed to cut between two little clamps. It's not difficult to do *(it feels a bit like cutting a rubbery rope)*, but it is surreal. There's a moment of hesitation, and then *snip* — you've officially participated in your first parental task. Don't worry, the baby doesn't feel a thing.

Announcing the gender: If you opted not to find out ahead of time, and if your medical team agrees, they might let you be the one to take a look and share the news. It's one of those small, unforgettable details you'll be talking about for years. Just make sure you take a second to be absolutely sure before shouting the results of your analysis.

Helping to catch the baby: If things are uncomplicated and your provider is comfortable with it, they might guide your hands and let you help bring your baby into the world. You'll be coached through it, helped the entire way, and reminded — *frequently* — to hold tight and stay calm. Helping deliver your child can be an overwhelming experience in the best possible way. It's messy, emotional, and very surreal. And it places you squarely in the moment, right at the threshold of this new chapter in your life.

So if you're thinking about being more involved, *do it!*

Just don't drop anything slippery.

The Moment

The doctor will say — *"One more big push!"* — and suddenly a messy, squirming, surprisingly purple, pointy-headed little person emerges into the world.

The sound of that first cry hit me like a physical force. I was laughing and crying simultaneously, a complete emotional mess, while the medical professionals calmly went about their business as if they hadn't just witnessed an actual miracle.

My wife, who had been working so incredibly hard, collapsed back against the pillows with an expression I'll never forget—exhaustion, relief, joy, and a kind of fierce triumph all mixed together.

"It's a girl," the doctor announced, and just like that, our daughter was placed on my wife's chest, still covered in the evidence of her journey, eyes squinted against the bright new world.

Time stopped. Everything — the discomfort of the past hours, the anxiety, the fear, all of the innumerable struggles and confusion of the last 9 months — all of it vanished in an instant. There was only this moment. This tiny person. This new reality.

First Embrace

I won't lie — holding our baby for the first time was both the most incredible and the most terrifying thing I've ever done.

They're so small. Like, shockingly small. They don't do much yet, but somehow, they feel like the most important thing in the universe. You will probably cry. Even if you don't think you're the type. Everything leading up to this moment will feel like a blur. But this? This sticks with you forever.

When the nurse finally placed my little girl in my arms, I was struck by how impossibly light she was. How could something so small come with such an enormous weight of responsibility? Her little face was scrunched up, her eyes barely open, and her hands were curled into tiny fists.

Then she yawned — this impossibly small, perfect yawn — and I was done for. Tears were happening. Lots of them. In front of everyone.

And I didn't care at all because I was holding my daughter.

Welcome to Fatherhood

The baby is here.

Your life? *Changed.*

The birth, as monumental, exhausting, and emotional as it was, is just the opening chapter to an entirely new story. What comes next is the sleepless nights, the first smiles, the countless diapers, the moments of doubt, and the deepest, most soul-penetrating love that you've ever experienced.

You will continue to make mistakes — as you should. That just means you're learning. You will have moments of brilliance. You will be tested in ways you never imagined. You will discover strength you didn't know you had. And through it all, you'll watch this tiny human you helped create begin to grow into a person.

It's terrifying. It's incredible. It's fatherhood.

Welcome to the club, my friend.

THE FOURTH TRIMESTER

Welcome to the fourth trimester — the rarely mentioned sequel to pregnancy where the baby is out, the sleep is gone, and the stakes have never felt higher.

You'll be exhausted. You'll be overwhelmed. You may, at some point, put your phone in the fridge, wear the same shirt for three days, or briefly forget how to make toast.

But this is also when the magic really starts. You'll feel the weight of your child's head against your chest. You'll see them calm at the sound of your voice. You'll learn how to change a diaper one-handed while mentally calculating how long it's been since you last showered.

You've officially entered the most chaotic, tender, humbling, and wildly important season of your life.

Welcome to it!

Chapter 11

New Baby

It's selfish, I know, but of all the new-parent anxieties I had developed, sleep disturbances ranked near the top — just beneath *"dropping the baby."* This was, in large part, due to the fact that every new parent I spoke to seemed to have a horror story of how their baby mercilessly grenaded their sleep. The dad-shaped-shell-of-a-human at work who hadn't slept through the night in seven months. The depleted mother whose newborn refuses to sleep unless firmly latched to her nipple. I listened politely to these cautionary tales, nodded with feigned empathy, and prayed that we would somehow be the exception.

You can imagine our utter astonishment when, on her very first night in the world, our daughter Molly slept all the way through it. Not a stir. Not a whimper. Just deep, calm, silent, peaceful, uninterrupted slumber.

We couldn't believe it.

Tambi, already feeling the heavy weight of maternal responsibility, must have checked on the baby a dozen times that night. *"She's so still,"* her whispered voice tight with a blend of awe and concern. I joined her now and then, the two of us standing quietly in the soft glow of the nightlight, staring into the bassinet with the dazed disbelief of people who couldn't quite believe the baby was real — let alone that she was actually sleeping through the night.

Had we actually won the infant lottery?

The following night provided an answer to that question:

Nope.

Night two was when Molly formally introduced herself. Turns out that the first night was less a gift and more a trap. A false story told by a freshly birthed infant who had, perhaps, been too exhausted from the trauma of being evicted upon expiration of her nine-month lease. Once she'd sufficiently recharged, she made it quite clear that she was not, in fact, a sleep-through-the-night-type-baby. She was a standard-issue, sleep-depriving newborn. Which meant we were standard-issue, sleep-deprived parents.

From that second night forward, we joined the multitudes of bleary-eyed initiates in the great fraternity of nocturnal parenting. We slept in 90-minute increments. We took shifts. We developed an unspoken system of silent handoffs, like midnight Olympic relay runners. Naps became currency. Coffee became fuel. I began to refer to our new rhythm as *"werewolf hours,"* and it felt accurate, particularly in the way that the sudden shift in priorities would result in Tambi going a full 8 weeks without shaving her legs.

The most peculiar effect of sleep deprivation, I discovered, was its impact on my short-term memory. Entire conversations would vanish from my mind as if they had never happened. Tambi would refer to plans we had apparently made, and I would stare at her blankly, wondering if she was playing a practical joke.

"Your parents are coming over this afternoon," she said.

"They are?" I replied, baffled. *"When did we discuss this?"*

"We talked about it while you were eating cereal this morning."

"I ate cereal this morning?"

It was as if I had developed a form of amnesia that specifically targeted any information exchanged while in a state of sleep-deprived stupor, which, as of late, accounted for roughly 97% of my *"waking"* hours.

Was it difficult? *Yep.*

Was it worth it? *Yep.*

I still think back to that first miraculous night. The quiet. The stillness. The audacity of hope. We were duped, of course — masterfully so. But in hindsight, I'm grateful for the ruse. That one perfect night gave Tambi the rest she desperately needed and gave me just enough of a fantasy to briefly believe I'd sidestepped the age-old curse of sleepless new parenthood. For twelve short hours, I believed we were chosen. Then, like every parent before me, I resigned myself to the paternity of the perpetually pooped.

Meconium

When they mention meconium in the baby books, it's usually in the context of it being a unique variety of excrement that a newborn will produce during its first few days of life. This is factually true, but what the books fail to mention is that it is actually not poo in any familiar sense of the word. It is a dark, tar-like substance that will emerge from your precious baby within a few days of birth. It has the adhesion strength of industrial sealant. Its color palette runs the spectrum between green and black. It's sticky, it's dense, and it defies logic, gravity, and most known laws of physics.

Our first encounter with the stuff happened on the 3rd morning of being new parents. Little Molly was asleep, and the room was peaceful. Dappled sunlight streamed through the curtains. Soft lullaby music was playing, and the faint smell of lavender hung in the air. It was a picture-perfect scene of familial serenity.

Then we heard a slow, wet, thick, bubbly sound.

Now, I'm no pushover when it comes to messes. I've dealt with marine grease that sticks to everything, mud that smells like ancient soup, and chemicals that melt paint from farm equipment. I don't flinch at filth. But, to me, there's something uniquely unsettling about an organic substance that has *oozed* from a human body.

Regardless, we had mentally prepared for this moment. We approached the task at hand as if it were a military operation. Wipes, diapers, backup clothes, and a changing pad — all strategically positioned to help ensure a successful outcome of the mission at hand.

Tambi gently lifted Molly's legs while I carefully unfastened the tiny diaper. What we found inside looked like a substance that would be at home on the hull of a shipwreck. Greenish-black, unnaturally glossy, and somehow both watery and glue-like at the same time. I grabbed the inaugural wipe of what would eventually become a cumulative total of 874,239, and approached the goo with caution.

I wiped. It smeared. I wiped again. It mocked me. The tenacious substance latched onto every surface it was within close proximity of. Additionally, it seemed to possess regenerative qualities, multiplying itself the more I tried to remove it. But, eventually, after what felt like a full hour and several dozen wipes, little Molly was squeaky clean. Tambi and I high-fived. We fitted a fresh diaper with great ceremony and pride. Our first meconium diaper was behind us, and we were victorious.

And then, just as I was snapping the final button of Molly's onesie — we heard a slow, wet, thick, bubbly sound.

Same goo. Same horror. It was as if she'd been waiting for the moment we let our guard down. Tambi and I just stared at each other in silence. We didn't speak. We didn't need to. We both knew what we had to do, so we got to work.

That's the thing about meconium. It's not a one-time event. It keeps coming for a day or two. Each diaper change is a fresh round of personal reflection and scientific discovery. Mercifully, it quickly transitions into what pediatricians call *"transitional stool,"* which sounds like a place to sit while you're waiting for a place to sit, but it's really just a somewhat less other-worldly version of the same weird poo. Eventually, after a few more days, you enter the world of normal baby poo, which you will one day regard with the same reverence as one might welcome spring after a long, harsh winter.

Action Steps

Congratulations! You've survived birth and brought home a tiny human who has absolutely no respect for your sleep schedule. Here's what needs your attention during the first month of parenthood:

Create your sleep survival strategy. Newborn sleep patterns are designed by nature to break the human spirit. Accept now that no one will be getting solid sleep for a while, then develop tactical approaches to minimize the damage.

Implement sleep shifts where possible. Perhaps you take the 8 PM to 1 AM shift while your partner sleeps, then switch. Master the art of the power nap. Even 20 minutes at a time can make a big difference. Create optimal sleep conditions: blackout curtains, white noise machines, and a "*sleep when the baby sleeps*" mindset that prioritizes rest over household tasks. Learn safe co-sleeping guidelines if that's your preference, or establish a bassinet setup that minimizes disruption during night feedings. Use nightlights for feedings rather than overhead lights, prep overnight diaper stations so you're not hunting for supplies at 3 AM, and keep a snack and water station by feeding areas.

This isn't about perfectly solving newborn sleep challenges. Instead, it's about developing systems that allow your family to function despite them.

Establish your postpartum support infrastructure. I'm typically a reasonably self-sufficient type of person, but the "*it takes a village*" concept exists for a reason. Humans aren't designed to care for newborns without a bit of community support. If friends and family offer help, direct them with specificity: "*We could really use a home-cooked meal on Tuesday*" is far more effective than "*Sure, anything helps.*" Set up a meal train using online platforms where people can sign up for specific dates.

Hire postpartum support if financially possible — even a few hours of a postpartum doula, night nurse, or house cleaner can be sanity-saving. We didn't do this, of course, but it sounds like a nice luxury if it's in the cards.

Create visitor guidelines that support rather than deplete your family. Short visits, helping with a specific task, bringing food, and understanding if you need to cut things short for feeding or naps. Don't hesitate to postpone visitors who won't genuinely help.

Remember that support isn't just for your partner. You're also adjusting to massive life changes and deserve assistance. The strongest fathers aren't those who do everything alone; they're the ones wise enough to accept help so they can be present and effective for their families.

Master essential newborn safety skills. Your protective instincts are in high gear, but they need to be paired with practical knowledge. Take an infant CPR and choking class. Many hospitals offer these. Learn the proper technique for taking a newborn's temperature *(hint: it's not under the arm)*. Understand safe sleep guidelines thoroughly: back to sleep, no blankets or soft items in the sleeping area, appropriate room temperature, and recognizing SIDS risk factors. Create a first-aid kit specifically for infant needs. Install your car seat correctly and have it checked by a certified inspector — then learn how to secure your baby in it properly.

These skills aren't just about being prepared for emergencies; they're about developing the confidence to care for your vulnerable newborn *AND* drastically reducing your own anxiety. Knowledge directly reduces fear, allowing you to enjoy parenthood with a feeling of preparedness, rather than just surviving it day to day.

Create intentional self-care practices for <u>both</u> parents. The myth that good parents sacrifice everything for their children is stupid. That practice leads to burnout, relationship strain, and diminished parenting ability.

Take care of yourselves by establishing simple, realistic self-care rituals that preserve your identity beyond *"baby care machine."* For each parent, identify one non-negotiable daily practice *(a shower, 15 minutes alone, a short walk)* and protect that time fiercely. Schedule slightly longer breaks weekly — perhaps an hour where each of you gets complete freedom from baby duty to exercise, connect with friends, or simply stare at a wall in blessed silence.

Watch for signs of postpartum depression and anxiety in both parents. Fathers can experience postpartum mood disorders, too, though they're less commonly recognized. Create space for regular check-ins about mental health, relationship needs, and individual well-being. These aren't selfish indulgences; they're essential maintenance that allows you to parent sustainably.

Chapter 12
The Beginning

You began this journey months ago, wide-eyed and bewildered — perhaps staring doubtfully at a recently peed-upon plastic stick. You've since navigated morning sickness, mood swings, nesting marathons, prenatal appointments, and the ever-changing ecosystem that is pregnancy. You've survived. You've adapted. And whether you know it or not, you've grown by leaps and bounds.

You may not feel like a *"good dad"* yet, and that's entirely okay. But because you've taken this book to heart — the advice, the stories, the cautionary tales — you're already well ahead of the curve. You've proven that you're the kind of dad who carries the weight of fatherhood, not because it's easy, but because it's one of the highest honors and privileges that a man can have.

Now your focus shifts to new challenges that will have you sleep-deprived, confused, amazed, overwhelmed, and occasionally pooped on, often all in the same hour. But you'll also experience moments that will rearrange your soul. The first time they wrap their tiny fingers around yours. The first smile. The first giggle. The first time they settle when you're holding them. These are the things that cement the title of *"good dad"* deep into your bones.

And that's why this isn't the end — *it's the beginning.*

The next chapter of your journey is the first year of your baby's life. That's when the real lessons kick in. How to soothe a screaming newborn at 3 AM. How to change a diaper one-handed in a public restroom. How to keep a marriage alive when you're both running on fumes. And how not to miss the countless moments of joy in the midst of the mess.

Being a *good dad* isn't about being perfect. It's about being there. Every day. In big ways and small ones. It's about laughing when things go sideways, learning from your mistakes, and choosing to stay in the game even when you're exhausted, unsure, or wearing a shirt that smells vaguely of spit-up.

Keep up the *good* work, and I'll talk to you again soon!

~ Ben

www.ingramcontent.com/pod-product-compliance
Lightning Source LLC
Chambersburg PA
CBHW071406120626
46546CB00002B/839